AF225970

"A resounding wake-up call to men who want to be allies to women and not just lip-service supporters! Thank you, Todd Korpi, for pointing the way with humility, grace, and humor for what it will look like for men and women to be true partners in the gospel."

—SHEILA WRAY GREGOIRE, FOUNDER OF BAREMARRIAGE.COM

"Todd Korpi is a voice of healing to every woman who has been disempowered because of her gender. This book takes you on an informative, engaging, and empowering journey. Korpi gives spiritual and intellectual depth to the pain women in ministry have wrestled with for centuries. His transparency moved me, and his practical examples and strategies gave me hope for the future. *Your Daughters Shall Prophesy* is groundbreaking and culture-shifting."

—PETRA SCOTT, PRESIDENT AND CEO, THE ROAD TO JERUSALEM

"In *Your Daughters Shall Prophesy* you will find powerful practical insights on how to bring change. We need to employ Passover power, instead of Babel power, if we want to move beyond diversity, equity, and inclusion towards true empowerment of the women in our lives and in our churches. This book is truly a must-read with lots of eye-openers!"

—SEBASTIAAN VAN WESSEM, LEAD PASTOR, CELEBRATION CHURCH NETHERLANDS

"*Your Daughters Shall Prophecy* is a much-needed resource for the church. It is a powerful and inspiring resource that offers practical strategies for empowering women to lead, minister, and serve in their communities. Todd Korpi approaches challenging theological issues with sensitivity and a deep understanding of the biblical foundations for gender equality. As co-pastoring leaders, this work is near and dear to our hearts. Put this book at the top of your reading list."

—TIM AND JEN TIMBERLAKE, SENIOR PASTORS, CELEBRATION CHURCH JACKSONVILLE, FL

"This latest contribution by Todd Korpi to the relevant conversation regarding the shared role of women as equals with men in relation to the full expression of the kingdom of God is nothing short of masterful. There are many books being written on women in ministry in the current milieu. I am persuaded that this one will have a lasting impact for generations to come. *Your Daughters Shall Prophesy* is an essential contribution to a crucial conversation."

—MARK J. CHIRONNA, FOUNDING AND LEAD PASTOR, CHURCH ON THE LIVING EDGE

"Todd Korpi is a pastor and a scholar. As a scholar, his work provides an engaging, thoughtful, and provocative challenge to the church, particularly male pastors. As a pastor, he recognized the significant leadership gift in his wife and took humble action steps to elevate her leadership voice ahead of his own in their church. He does not challenge men to walk where he has not already gone first. His book provides practical tools for those who want to support female leaders."

—ANNA MORGAN, LEAD PASTOR, WORD OF LIFE CHURCH

"In *Your Daughters Shall Prophesy*, Todd Korpi deftly and sensibly navigates context and biblical narrative surrounding the topic of women in ministry and egalitarianism. Through honest stories from his own life and marriage, along with those of others, Korpi challenges inconsistencies in one's support (rhetoric) and practice (action) regarding women in ministry. This book assists the reader in reimagining life in Christ in an egalitarian manner both in the home and church."

—KATJA AND PHIL ZARNS, CO-CREATORS OF ECLECTIC EGALITARIAN

"The lived experience of women in the church is too often marked by men who are either ambivalent or openly hostile to their roles. Men, like Todd Korpi, have the credentials and the insight to make the case for women's leadership where often women making that same case are dismissed. Korpi's work cannot be ignored as he presents both the theological case and the practical benefits of women's leadership, influence, and service. This will be a book that pastors, lay people, and academics will value."

—JOY QUALLS, ASSOCIATE PROFESSOR OF COMMUNICATION STUDIES, BIOLA UNIVERSITY

Your Daughters Shall Prophesy

Your Daughters Shall Prophesy

Amplifying the Voice and Place of Christian Women

TODD KORPI

WIPF & STOCK · Eugene, Oregon

YOUR DAUGHTERS SHALL PROPHESY
Amplifying the Voice and Place of Christian Women

Copyright © 2023 Todd Korpi. All rights reserved. Except for brief quotations in critical publications or reviews, no part of this book may be reproduced in any manner without prior written permission from the publisher. Write: Permissions, Wipf and Stock Publishers, 199 W. 8th Ave., Suite 3, Eugene, OR 97401.

Wipf & Stock
An Imprint of Wipf and Stock Publishers
199 W. 8th Ave., Suite 3
Eugene, OR 97401

www.wipfandstock.com

PAPERBACK ISBN: 978-1-6667-4764-5
HARDCOVER ISBN: 978-1-6667-4765-2
EBOOK ISBN: 978-1-6667-4766-9

03/27/23

Scripture quotations from the COMMON ENGLISH BIBLE. © Copyright 2011 COMMON ENGLISH BIBLE. All rights reserved. Used by permission. (www.CommonEnglishBible.com).

To Mark and Michele Benson
For pioneering the egalitarian way that Tara and I have walked

Contents

Acknowledgments

I am deeply indebted and forever grateful to the host of support, feedback, prayer, and help I received throughout the course of writing this book. To Petra Scott, who provided helpful feedback and encouragement in this whole process. To Dr. Anna Morgan, for most excellent insight into female leadership and for your and John's example of egalitarian pastoring. To the numerous female clergy who shared your stories of both triumph and difficulty in ministry. To Bishop Mark Chironna, whose friendship came at a most providential time and whose wisdom and encouragement during the writing of this book was indispensable.

And, of course, my beloved wife, the Rev. Tara Korpi. Your honest feedback and support (both in prayer and practically) made this book possible. My prayer is that the hard soil you have tilled in ministry will be fertile land for our daughters in the years to come, so that they may reap the rewards of all you have labored. Thank you for walking this life alongside me.

To Lydia, to Anna, and to Benson, three very different but very beautiful pictures of feminine beauty and strength. This book is because of you. I'm proud to be your father.

CHAPTER 1

Great Expectations

"Would this be different if I wasn't a woman?"

Tara sat to my right at a small, round table in our senior pastor's office on a hot August afternoon in Tulsa, Oklahoma. The youth pastor at our church sat on the other side of her, arms folded in indignation. She levied the question to our senior pastor who sat directly across from her with a countenance that was one part frustration and another, resignation.

I was seething with anger when I heard him suggest that Tara should step down as the associate youth pastor to become my secretary. We arrived in Tulsa in June 2008, only two months earlier, after returning from our honeymoon. Originally, only I was interviewed for the position of children's pastor at the church. But the senior pastor, upon discovering that Tara also felt a calling to be a pastor, offered her a job as associate youth pastor. We were elated at the prospect that our first ministry position would allow us *both* to be in the pastorate full-time!

But after a few weeks following our arrival to the church, we began to wonder whether we made a mistake. The youth pastor's treatment toward Tara was severe and unrelenting. Despite the best attempts that a twenty-two-year-old newlywed straight out of Bible college could muster, she simply could not please the man. It all finally came to a head that afternoon when the youth pastor demanded the senior pastor remove Tara from his department. There was no moral failure, no financial misdoing, and no outlandish behavior toward a member of the congregation. In fact, only a few days before this fateful meeting, it was *she* who was the subject of a loud and aggressive verbal lashing from *him* in front of the youth while on a youth group trip to Six Flags. But his conduct was not on trial.

The absence of empirical evidence of Tara's wrongdoing to justify the youth pastor's behavior—and the pastor's insistence that she not be fired but instead be reassigned to become my secretary—ultimately brought Tara to the point of asking her direct question: *"Would this be different if I wasn't a woman?"*

When the words left her mouth, I was surprised by the silliness of the question. Surely, if it *was* because she was a woman, nobody in their right mind would admit it! But how could her gender be the issue? After all, we were both serving at an egalitarian church which boasted egalitarian theology.[1] After all, it was the senior pastor who had proactively offered her the job. What a ridiculous notion.

But to my surprise, the pastor sheepishly retorted, "yeah, probably."

I was stunned.

We were serving in a church that was a part of the Pentecostal tradition—a tradition that was ordaining women to be pastors when my great-grandfather was still in diapers. I simply could not wrap my mind around the fact that, without any specified wrongdoing, such a blanket dismissal of her calling could be so explicitly offered.

And what was I to do? I was twenty-two and naïve. I had already been rebuked several times for voicing my intolerance for the manner in which Tara was being treated during that summer. What was my place? Should I defend her? Should I keep my own mouth shut so that she could defend herself? In one instant, the egalitarian bubble in which we were trained to be ministers was burst, and I was left with the simultaneous feelings of rage and indescribable sorrow. I felt that stepping in front of her to fight for her was disempowering of her, but staying silent was cowardly.

Rather than accept Tara's reassignment, we ultimately decided to leave the church after two-and-a-half months in ministry and return to our home state of Michigan. We were supervised by a tearful board member as we cleaned out our offices over a weekend while no one else was in the building, as though we were being dismissed for theft. The board gave us a $10,000 severance, and the pastor told us we weren't allowed to speak to anyone in the congregation about the matter. This was before it was commonplace for churches to coerce departing employees to sign non-disclosure agreements, but one wasn't needed—we were young and thought that we would be finished in ministry if we let people know the truth of what happened.

---

1. Egalitarianism is the theological belief that women and men are called by God as co-equals and, as it pertains to church ministry, both can hold the office of pastor.

We later heard from a congregant, offended by our departure, that the pastor told the congregation we had come by a "large sum of money" and decided to move back home.

As we packed up the moving truck by ourselves the following week, I was dumbfounded at how such a series of events could transpire. How could a church *teach* that women should be in ministry but treat a woman in ministry so poorly? We wound up returning to my home city of Flint, where we struggled to regain our footing during the advent of the Great Recession. It was here, while attending my home church, that we began to further realize how egalitarianism—the theological affirmation that women can be pastors—may not be all that we thought it was cracked up to be.

Unbeknownst to us, Tara's experience of gender discrimination in our first post in ministry was not uncommon, both among the female pastors with whom we trained in Bible college or female pastors and leaders throughout the broader church. One such story we only recently came to hear happened around the same time of our experience in Tulsa. A husband and wife pastoral duo who attended Bible college with us (I will call the wife Angela, though that's not her name[2]) took a ministry post in Missouri. Armed with the same zealous passion for the gospel, these newlyweds relocated to serve at a mid-sized church within our denomination. Both held ministerial credentials, though it was her husband who was on the payroll. Angela recalled the summary of her first experience in this new church:

> On our first Sunday my husband and I sat on the front row of a brightly lit, pleasant sanctuary with wooden pews. After worship I [took] out my journal to take sermon notes. The pastor announced what his new sermon series would be: "Gender Roles & The Church"
>
> . . . I put my pen down . . . and as I listened, I turned my head to glance back at the congregants to visually confirm [whether] they were tracking with this message. No resistance. This went on for weeks. The pastor went on about passages in the Bible where women are to be silent. What women should wear. How women aren't to teach a man. . .
>
> This pastor boasted how he made it his goal to take female pastors to lunch and convince them they had missed their call. I sat amazed . . . paralyzed. I had just moved 12 hours from my family with a degree & credential that matched my husband's, but I would never be able to be fully myself in this space. I

2. Throughout this book, I use pseudonyms for most of the testimonies of women I share. I have done this out of a desire to let their experiences be heard while protecting the stability of their vocations.

learned quickly that my husband would be "pastor" but that title couldn't accompany my name. . .[3]

Angela's story continued with details of spiritual abuse, specifically focused upon the women of this so-called egalitarian church. The pastor would call in the female custodian, who lived twenty miles away, to come and pick up a single wad of paper on the floor of the foyer. When it was reported to the pastor that a man in the church was abusing his wife, the pastor refused to believe her. Eventually he was dismissed for this spiritual abuse by the church. This inaugurated a journey for Angela trying to find her voice in churches that ultimately tried to silence her or relegate her into a corner, teaching only other women. For both Angela and her husband, for Tara and I, as well as many others in our acquaintance, vocational ministry has been marked by a dizzying disconnect between what egalitarian churches and organizations *say* about women and what egalitarian churches and organizations *do* about women.

GROWING UP EGALITARIAN

Egalitarianism, a word that I will use throughout this book, is a theological position that claims women and men alike are called by God as co-equals and that both women and men can hold the office of pastor. Among egalitarians, there is some debate about *which* pastoral offices women can hold and how the co-equal status extends into the home (my position on both will become clear later).

I was the fourth generation in my family to be a member of the egalitarian Pentecostal church of my youth and the youngest member in the church's history to date. After my great-grandfather F. L. Strength retired from church planting and pastoring in New England, he settled his family in the city of Flint, which at the time was rapidly growing due to the boom of the automotive industry. My grandmother was a strong, independent sort, who eventually became the Sunday school superintendent of the church. My mother herself taught Sunday school throughout my childhood and often preached at churches, Bible studies, and women's groups around eastern Michigan.

All the while, my father modeled to me the reserved stoicism that is stereotypical of his Finnish-American upbringing, coupled with a strong support of my mother in her teaching and preaching endeavors. Though a deacon for years in our church, he brewed and served coffee for the adult

3. Personal correspondence, Oct 27, 2022.

students (men and women alike) who would attend my mother's classes. In my childhood I never saw what many of the "theobros"[4] on social media attempt to portray—that the empowerment of women must necessarily result in the weakening of men. Quite the contrary, actually. I observed that my father's inner strength and authority was best showcased in its use to support my mother's calling. It wasn't until I became much older that I realized that there were Christian men—with followings amassed of all sizes—who fancy themselves macho through their penchant for keeping women under an ecclesial lid. For a man to feel the need to constantly remind women of "their place" didn't seem especially masculine to me (it still doesn't), but there is certainly a market for it on the internet.

Growing up in the Pentecostal movement, strong women like Aimee Semple McPherson and Agnes Ozman were household names. Among Flint Pentecostals, the name of Sister Berniece Matejcek,[5] who pastored Faith Tabernacle for thirty-eight years and who performed over three thousand weddings, baptisms, and baby dedications during her ministry, was a woman who had reached almost a mythical status. She was, and remains, a legend among those who were around during her ministry. I knew there were Christian groups who didn't ordain women but didn't think much of it. I was raised to associate the practice of ordaining women with the fulfillment of Joel 2:28–29—that the Spirit would be poured out on men and women alike and that both our sons and our daughters would prophetically declare God's greatness, both in the church and to the outside world.

When I went to Bible college, I was immersed in an egalitarian perspective of both ministry and biblical interpretation. It is here that I met Tara and, after a couple years of friendship, became enraptured by her feminine strength and her heart for the gospel. She was (and remains) everything I hoped for in a wife: sensitive and strong, wise and bold, loving and independent, and a keen mind without any fear of applying it.

But when we got married, we quickly began to realize that neither the church, nor our marriage, were as idealistically egalitarian as we expected them to be. Our wave of newlywed expectations would soon be dashed against the rocks of reality.

4. A term commonly used in Twitter conversation for Christian men who argue at length in favor of patriarchy and mid-twentieth century white American cultural norms concerning masculinity.

5. "Obituaries: Berniece Matejcek."

UNMET EXPECTATIONS

Our experience in Tulsa, not only because of Tara's dismissal for being a woman, but also as newlyweds, caused me to begin to realize that egalitarianism is not as simple as I grew up believing. While our idealistic expectations for the church were dashed, there was also a great deal that existed within me that was *far* from egalitarian.

Yes, I grew up watching my mother teach Sunday School while my deacon father served coffee. But I did not know that my mother, and the other women of the church, were explicitly forbidden from serving in the deacon office my father held—despite biblical precedence for it (Rom 16:1). What's more, I grew up within a church that taught women *could* be pastors yet throughout its history had only hired white men.

We attended a wonderful Bible college that was aggressively pro-women, though it (innocently enough, I'm sure) failed to prepare us for the harsh reality that the broader tradition to which it belonged still was long in making strides toward a more equal playing field for women. While I learned about Aimee Semple McPherson and Agnes Ozman, it is because they were anomalies within a Pentecostal tradition whose power and authority was still largely concentrated with men. While the sentiments of a very small minority who harbored reservations about women in the pastorate in college seemed like an outlier, in the real world those sentiments were more mainstream, even among churches that gave lip service to women in ministry, as both Tara's and Angela's experiences attested.

Two things are worth noting at the onset of this book. First, I believe that most egalitarian churches and egalitarian pastors do not consciously set up barriers for their female counterparts. Some certainly do intentionally build barriers. But many do so out of well-intentioned ignorance or through maintaining existing systems that make ministry extra-difficult for women without realizing it. This book is not intended to produce shame but rather conviction. It is my desire to elevate the experience of women—many whose stories I will share in the pages that follow—to bring awareness in egalitarian spaces that our theology of equality provides more of a cover to hide patriarchal practices that negatively impact the lives of women in our churches and in Christian organizations and which must be uprooted. It is only through amplifying the voice of women that we can hear the Spirit speaking through their prophetic voices and respond with change.

Second, I have perpetuated much of the same duplicity in my own life for which I make critique in this book. Not all, but many of topics covered in these chapters are born from my own shortcomings or those I have witnessed over the past fifteen years of pastoral ministry in egalitarian churches.

I have paid lip service to being the "most pro-women" of those who are pro-women-in-ministry, and yet I am guilty of setting up barriers for my own wife to flourish—and, I'm sure, other women as well. I entered ministry intentionally seeking out a partner like Tara who was strong, independent, and wanted to labor alongside me in pastoral ministry. Yet, when we were first married, I also expected her to do my ironing, shoulder most of the housework, and all of the cooking (more on that later). I wanted her to be in ministry, but I also implicitly expected her to drop whatever she was doing at a moment's notice to help me in whatever I was doing. We were theologically equal but functionally hierarchal. Much of this book is born from the womb of my own foolish mistakes as a pastor's husband. I've embarked upon the journey of facing the patriarchy laden under the surface of my loud egalitarian beliefs and have exorcised it for the sake of my wife's calling and for the sake of the gospel. Though certainly, there is more work to be done in me.

FACING MY PATRIARCHY

While I quickly learned that I could not import the household expectations of ironing, cooking, and cleaning that I grew up observing, it took me much longer to see just how deep the depths of patriarchy can run in even the most egalitarian heart. Simply because you are passionately in support of female pastors, it doesn't mean you do not possess patriarchal properties deep within. While Tara and I had the typical squabbles that many couples who co-lead together in ministry have (many of which will be described in this book), it wasn't until we planted a church in *my* home city, that I began to see just how much work I had to do in my own heart.

It was in late 2013 that Tara and I began dreaming and strategizing what it would look like to plant a church in Flint, Michigan. Before we got married, we both felt a call (separately, I might add) to begin a new church in a city that boasted some of the most difficult problems among American cities—unrelenting violence, deindustrialization, shrinking population, poverty, poor education—and eventually a lead-in-water crisis that brought Flint to the national stage just as we were launching our church.

Throughout the process of preparing to plant and eventually pastoring the church, however, I found myself giving lip service to Tara's part in the whole endeavor while harboring a distinct and unrelenting sense that if the *city* were mine then so must the *church* be, too. Because I was born from the grease and grime of Flint, I must naturally be the *de facto* head, though we could call ourselves co-pastors. In those first few years of pastoring together, I found myself hoarding vision, ignoring her input, and at times running ahead without her. She became a figurehead in her own church because my pride could not stand to share with her any glory that might come.

You can certainly hear the pride in this posture as you read. I can scarcely stand to put it on paper without wincing. But it's the truth. And it wasn't until a couple years into pastoring together, with the help of the example of Wilmer Villacorta, who was the cohort mentor of my master's program at Fuller Theological Seminary, that I began to realize that I was content with Tara flourishing in her calling—but there was a lid on it. She could only flourish insofar as it didn't inconvenience *my* calling. She could shine insofar as she didn't outshine *me*. Through his example, Wilmer modeled to me what it looked like to move beyond a passive *supporter* of women in ministry to a passionate *advocate*. This necessarily requires that we men model our conduct toward our female contemporaries after the posture of Jesus.

Jesus—dare I say, the epitome of godly masculinity—advocated for Mary's right to sit at his feet. He defended the woman who was caught in the act of adultery. He ignored societal expectations to lift the voice of women like the woman with the issue of blood and the Samaritan woman at the well. He sat and ate with prostitutes.

What's more, God saw fit for a woman to, through her womb, be the first to carry the Gospel. It was women who first proclaimed the news of the resurrected Christ. It was a woman who discipled Apollos (Acts 18:26). It was a woman who was entrusted with housing one of the first churches in Europe (Acts 16:11–40).

If men—especially those of us who claim to support women in ministry—are to embrace a godly posture toward our female co-laborers, we must move from a passive support toward a passionate advocacy. We must model ourselves after Jesus who stewarded his power for the benefit of those, including women, who are often cut off by systems of resistance from their God-given right to flourish.

WHY I'M WRITING THIS BOOK

This book is not as much an apologetic for women in ministry as it is a guide for how to support women in ministry. By this I mean that there are a host of wonderful resources already available from a host of great thinkers like Marg Mowczko, Scot McKnight, and Lucy Peppiatt who make the scriptural case for why women can and should be pastors. By contrast this book is unique in that it assumes that, if you're reading this, you already agree with that position to some extent (though if you do not agree, I invite you to prayerfully consider its contents nevertheless). While I spend a bit of time making a couple of arguments in favor of women in ministry, it is only a peripheral part of why this book exists.

Instead, I've observed that while there are scores of men who have a woman—be she a wife, daughter, staff member, or a friend—who is in vocational ministry, there are very few (if any) resources that exist that practically empower those men with wisdom to advocate for those women well. Instead, I've found that we tend to (out of blissful ignorance) repeatedly make some of the same mistakes because there isn't much out there to help us avoid doing so.

In chapters two and three of this book, I will explore the calling of a woman—why women not only *can* be pastors but why they *should* be. I'll also explore how women uniquely emerge in their calling and how that calling is different woman to woman.

In chapter four, I'll discuss how the issue of power stewardship is at the heart of what it means to amplify the voice of women. Chapter five will outline ways in which well-meaning supporters of women actually sometimes hurt in our attempt to help. Chapters six and seven will get into the nitty-gritty of the home, in which I will make a call to apply our same egalitarianism in the church in our homes and to broaden our view of healthy, egalitarian sexuality. Chapters eight and nine deal with phenomena women experience working in egalitarian churches and organizations. Finally, in chapter ten I will describe my heart for the future of women and the church.

A couple years ago while in the car with my oldest daughter (who was then eight years old), she randomly blurted out that she wanted to be a pastor like mommy when she grew up. At first, I welled up with pride and excitement. She would make a great pastor. She loves people and loves the Lord, and, while I know most parents say this about their kids, there's something special God has in store for her. But then an aching feeling inevitably followed as I recalled the 2008 conversation between my twenty-two-year-old wife and the senior pastor who told her she was to be demoted because she was a woman. I loathe the idea that something like that could happen to any of my three daughters.

But after the excitement—after the aching—a third feeling welled up within me as we drove through sunny Jacksonville, Florida, that day—*determination*. I was determined to trailblaze a clearer path in ministry for her. Fundamentally, that's what this book is meant to do. We must clear the path for my daughter—for all our daughters.

Chapter 2

The Daughters of the Church

OVER THE LAST FEW decades scores of resources have been written that address why an elevated, "egalitarian view" of the role of women should be embraced by the whole church. Most of these books and articles focus on an exegetical defense for the role of women, both in the church as well as in the home. While I will touch on some of these resources in this chapter, it is by no means meant to be an exhaustive and complete defense of the role of women, but rather an overview. I will recommend resources for further study where appropriate. At present, we will explore four lines of argumentation that are often overlooked regarding the role of women.

THE CREATION ARGUMENT

Often, when people want to talk about concepts such as male headship, the role of women in the church, and more, they turn to Paul. It is not Paul in a general sense, but rather a few "clobber verses" picked out of their textual and cultural context to insist upon a subservient vocational position of women in the church and at home.

Scripture, however, was not meant to be read as isolated bits of content, the way we pull a quote from the internet to post on social media. The Bible is not a Magic 8 Ball to which we ask a question and from which we derive a fortune-cookie answer. Instead, Scripture was meant to be read as a unified whole. It's a singular, Spirit-inspired story of God's redemptive purposes and plans for his creation—most of all, women and men. If this is true, what better place to start than at the very beginning? The creation narrative gives us a grand picture of God's vision for women.

I use the term "creation narrative" because that's precisely what Gen 1–3 is. A narrative—a *story*. It's not a science text from which we demand answers to modern scientific questions. In fact, Old Testament scholar John Walton notes that the story of creation was not even meant to tell the story of the *material* origins of the universe. Instead, when the ancients spoke about something coming into existence, they were referring to its *functional* origins—that is, how it was set apart for a purpose.[1] Genesis 1–3, Walton notes, is the story of the origins of creation's *purpose*, not its material origins. That does not mean God did not materially create the universe. It only means that this is not the point of the story the author of Genesis is trying to tell his audience. Instead, he's trying to describe the purpose for which all things were made.

While we're on the subject of how the ancients wrote, it's also important that we understand a significant difference between our culture (in the West) and the cultures of the Bible as it pertains to the content of a story. In the West, we live in a culture formed by the scientific precision that came out of the Enlightenment. We tell stories chronologically, the way we would describe the story while on the stand in a courtroom. Therefore, we place tremendous value on the correct chronological order with which things transpire and the historical accuracy of the details.

By contrast, the ancients (and many of the cultures in the global South and East today) are relational cultures. The point an author was trying to make to his or her audience mattered more than the scientific accuracy of the details. Authors would rearrange chronology or details to communicate an underlying truth. While we place value on the accuracy of a story, the ancients valued the message of a story.[2] This is why some of the details of the creation story don't always make scientific sense, such as how "light" was created on the first day, yet the sun, moon, and stars were not created until the fourth day.

Let's recap. First, Gen 1–3 is about the origins of creation's purpose. Second, it was intentionally structured by its ancient author to communicate a truth about that purpose. So, what does that tell us about women?

1. Walton, *Lost World of Adam and Eve*, 35–45; see also Walton, *Lost World of Genesis One*.

2. For more on this see Richards and O'Brien, *Misreading Scripture with Western Eyes*; Georges, *3D Gospel*.

Women in the Created Order

First, let's speak to the structure of the story of woman. Genesis 1 ends with a surface level description of humankind's origins, which probably includes both men and women. As the story progresses, we read about an ever-increasing complexity in creation as YHWH sets to order what he has brought into "existence" (i.e., set apart for its function). We begin with an expansive, empty void where nothing has been assigned function.[3] Then, the great Maestro begins to put his cosmic concerto together. First light and darkness, followed by sky, land, vegetation on that land, and celestial objects to oversee the land. Then he set apart life both in the depths of water and in the heights of the sky. Then land animals. And finally, humankind was set apart to its purpose. That purpose was to bear God's image, his likeness to creation. This requires that we steward creation on his behalf, in his wisdom, and in reflection of his glory. Part of that image-bearing vocation is also to reside as priests over creation, calling attention to the one who rules over all—beckoning all of creation to worship the one true God.[4]

But keep in mind that, in its original form, Genesis had no chapter and verse markers. Those came thousands of years later. Instead, the story continues straight away into what we know as chapter two, telling more specifically the manner by which man and woman were set apart. Again, it bears repeating that this creation story is not a scientific textbook but a story about humanity's purpose in relationship to God. So when we get to chapter two's description of the creation of humankind, we find that the complexity thread continues, first in the creation of Adam. Then, as the crown jewel of all of creation, God created woman.

This doesn't speak to woman's place in any hierarchy that might be assumed onto the scriptural story, but it speaks to something unique about woman, a manner in which she is unique in the created order. While it is only my opinion, I would suggest that this uniqueness is in the nature of the complexity and mystery of womanhood.

I don't mean complexity and mystery in the way that a husband might joke about not being able to understand his wife. By complexity and mystery I refer to the unquantifiable depths to womanhood that is unlike anything else in creation. I'm not referring to any particular set of "feminine characteristics." Notions of femininity have changed with the passing of time and are different between cultures around the world. But there is a sort

---

3. Walton et al., *IVP Bible Background Commentary*, 28.

4. Korpi, *Life-Giving Spirit*, 35–47; cf. Heiser, *Unseen Realm*, 40–43; Walton et al., *IVP Bible Background Commentary*, 29; Walton, *Lost World of Adam and Eve*, 104–15.

of universal complexity and mystery to womanhood—in particular in her ability to steward the cultivation of human life within her womb, that is both complex and mysterious in its own way.

That's not a bug; it's a feature. And it's beautiful.

Co-Priests of Sacred Space

Walton notes how we often read the creation of Eve through modern, Western eyes. When we see that Adam was put into a deep sleep (Gen 2:21), we assume it's something like a divine dose of anesthesia. But the action word there refers to a vision. Additionally, Walton also makes the argument (and I agree) that the word "side" is likely a better translation than "rib" in 2:21–22.[5] This is important.

Remembering that the story is about origins of *purpose*, not origins of *matter*. Both Adam and Eve likely already existed. But YHWH is giving Adam a vision in order to describe his wife's purpose. At some point previously, God already spoke her into existence. Now he will commission her, pronouncing *why* she exists.

Consequently, God gives Adam a vision wherein he sees himself split in two. From one of those halves, he sees Eve. In response to the waking vision, he exclaims "Bone of my bone! Flesh of my flesh!" (2:23) He recognizes her equal status and purpose. She is to him, and to creation, as he is.

It is providential that we see a similar prophetic vision in Matt 1, wherein Joseph is given a vision whereby the angel of the Lord appears and describes the purpose for which Mary, his betrothed, has been set apart. In the same manner the first Eve was set apart to steward the life that would come from her womb, the "Second Eve" was set apart to steward the New Life that would come from hers.

Eve receives the same creation mandate as Adam, to preside over and expand the sacred space of the garden into the rest of creation. That she is a "helper" to him is not a subservient role nor is it an administrative one.[6] *Together*, they are to function as co-priests of sacred space. The interdependent and co-equal priestly status of woman and man not only applies to their image-bearing status but to their vocational and missional status as well. Craig Keener notes,

> The historic reason that was traditionally given for rejecting women's ministry was that women were considered ontologically

5. Walton, *Lost World of Adam and Eve*, 77–79.
6. Imes, "Helper."

inferior to men. So if we reject the reason, then we probably ought to reject the conclusion too.[7]

We would do well to heed Keener's conclusion. If we can agree that the historic justification for barring women from ministry was errant (as our survey of the Genesis account demonstrates), we must also reject the conclusion that has marginalized the female calling. If women and men were created ontologically equal, it follows that they too must be equal in every respect, including vocation. Eve's commission establishes a co-equal status and function between woman and man, though a distinction of personhood exists between them. This co-equal status continues into chapter three and is only undone by their sin and subsequent exile.

While certainly Eve is a participant in the sinful plot that damages their equality, we see Adam commit an often overlooked sin—a sin that continues throughout the bloodline of the first Adam to this very day—he *blames* the woman (3:11). He scapegoats her for his own sin.

Is it not this very sin of blaming women that we find so evident throughout human history that is the subject of so much of the modern #MeToo and #ChurchToo movements meant to convince society to believe women rather than blame them? The very action of blaming women for the sin of men, whether it be power and/or sex abuse by a church leader or the horrific practice of victim blaming or the scapegoating of a wife from her husband for any score of intermarital sins, is a sin that traces its roots back to Adam himself. And it was this blaming of woman that the unraveling of the co-equal status of men and women began.

Reversing the Curse

As a result of Adam and Eve's sinfulness, God pronounced judgment upon them, often referred to as "the curse" or "the fall." This not only included their expulsion from Eden but for Eve, the promise of pain in childbirth and that she would "desire [her] husband, but he will rule over [her]" (3:16).

I've encountered some who argue for hierarchy between men and women to thereby exclaim, "Aha! See! It's right there, plain as day in Scripture!" And that's true. It *is* there, plain as day. The curse of original sin is that man would be destined to rule over woman instead of function equally alongside her. There it is indeed, codified in the very pages of Scripture itself for every macho man to lord over his subservient wife.

7. Keener, "Women in Ministry."

But in appealing to the curse of the fall as justification for patriarchy—for the right of men to rule over women—we must first reject the reversal of the curse by Jesus. Paul reminds us in 1 Cor 15 that the victory of Jesus won in his death and resurrection *reverses* this very curse of Gen 3. Paul notes that in the same way everyone dies (because of the curse) in the first Adam, in the second Adam (because of the reversal of the curse), we are to be made alive (15:20–22, 45). To suggest that Christ's victory was only a *partial* reversal is to do violence to the totality of the victory itself.[8] Embracing the fruit of the curse is incompatible with embracing the one who came to reverse the curse.

But the victory won by Jesus was complete and all-encompassing. Along with death, hell, and the grave, patriarchy was one of the victims of that victory. No longer is man to rule over woman. Rather, in Christ, those patriarchal bonds have been broken and woman is liberated to assume her rightful place—as co-priest, alongside man, stewarding the gospel in every place she goes.[9] This is precisely why the prophet Joel foretold that in the last days both sons *and* daughters would prophesy (Joel 2:28).

To cherry pick portions of sin's curse, such as patriarchy, that we'd prefer to maintain because doing so suits our preference for the status quo, undermines the very nature of the gospel message, which is to bind up those who are brokenhearted and liberate those who are held under oppression. And while the liberation of the oppressed has been (rightly) applied to various people groups throughout the history of the church, the liberation of women from patriarchy is perhaps the liberation most ignored throughout history, yet also the most blatantly clear in Scripture.

Genesis 3:16 was undone by John 3:16.

THE REDEMPTION ARC ARGUMENT

One of the things I love about the Bible is that it was written over such an expansive period of time. This is a benefit because its cohesion, despite differences between its authors in time, culture, language, and more, is a miracle in itself. This cohesive, grand story (called a "metanarrative") also allows us to see a bird's-eye view of how God's redemptive purposes have taken shape through his people (often imperfectly) over the course of time.

---

8. Foster, *Money, Sex & Power*, 106.

9. I owe my friend, Petra Scott, president of The Road to Jerusalem ministries, credit for this insight.

Regarding the equality between men and women, we can see a "redemptive arc"[10] take shape in the pages of Scripture as the story unfolds. It is a slow and steady evolution of Spirit-driven progress toward a redeemed version of what was intended at the beginning. After the creation narrative concludes with Adam and Eve's expulsion from the garden, the grip of patriarchy ensues. But we notice subtle, though significant shifts when we come to Exodus.

In Exod 20, Moses gives the newly liberated Hebrew people ten commandments from YHWH. As he describes these commandments to the people, he comes to the final one:

> Do not desire and try to take your neighbor's *house*. Do not desire and try to take your neighbor's *wife*, male or female servant, ox, donkey, or anything else that belongs to your neighbor (Exod 20:17, emphasis added).

That's a necessary list but kind of rough for our modern sensibilities, too. Remember, in the ancient world, the order in which things appeared in lists often spoke to its priority. In this listing *house* ranks first. The wife is listed with the servants, livestock and "anything else."

But fast-forward a generation and we come to Deuteronomy, where Moses is giving last instructions through a covenant renewal ceremony before Joshua succeeds him and marches the Hebrews into the land of Canaan. In Deut 5, Moses describes God's commandments again to them. But this time something changes:

> Do not desire and try to take your neighbor's *wife*. Do not crave your neighbor's *house*, field, male or female servant, ox, donkey, or anything else that belongs to your neighbor (Deut. 5:21, emphasis added).

The Exodus and Deuteronomy lists are identical. Identical except for one thing: the placement of women. Women come first in this second-generation list. Does this mean that there was a radical feminist uprising in the wilderness? Hardly. But it does signify that as the Hebrew people journeyed through their purgative wandering, guided by the Spirit of God, a little bit of Egypt wore off them and a little bit of YHWH wore off *on* them. In just one generation, women were elevated into a status not previously enjoyed in the land of Egypt.

Are women restored to their co-equal status? Not at all. But we do see the great feminine characters in the Jewish story emerge on the scene: Deborah, Hannah, Jael, Naomi and Ruth, Esther, etc. These are women who rose

---

10. I owe my good friend and Pauline scholar, Dr. John Phelps credit for this insight.

above culturally-mandated expectations to lead, to speak truth to power, to demonstrate uncommon godliness and virtue, and more. The Jewish story is marked by strong women rising to the occasion, defying cultural expectations, to obey God's call upon their lives.

When we turn to the New Testament, we see this redemptive arc continue. Mary is the one of the first principal figures to emerge on the scene. A young Jewish girl in Roman-occupied Galilee, she is entrusted with the very one who would be the salvation of Israel and all the nations of the world.

Luke draws out the prominence of women in his two-volume account of the ministry of Jesus and the continuing ministry of the infant church in Luke-Acts. Women are, in his account, the first to reach the empty tomb as well as the first preachers of the resurrection message (Luke 24:9–10). It should also be noted that the apostles committed the ancient Adamic error of failing to believe the women at first (24:11).

From Acts, Luke records the emergence of prominent women in the church that we see also in the writings of Paul. In Acts 16, Luke is careful to note that when in Philippi, Paul and the other people in his party sat down to talk with the women at the city gates, leading a cloth merchant named Lydia of Thyatira to become the first European convert to Christianity and the host of the first Philippian church in her home. Luke notes that the Lord enabled *her* (not her husband) to embrace Paul's message and move to have her household baptized (16:14–15).

From Acts, we witness prominent women emerge onto the scene in the infant church, enjoying a status not previously enjoyed in the outside Roman world. While Paul's "clobber passages" on gender get most of the attention, we actually see the ministry of the zealous apostle to be one that depended upon and interacted with strong women regularly. Paul is careful to mention these women, most often by name (implying significance) and most often absent of any mention of their association with their husbands (an uncommon practice in an otherwise patriarchal society). Lucy Peppiatt outlines this list of women who were in or around Paul's ministry in her book *Rediscovering Scripture's Vision for Women*:

- Tabitha (Acts 9:36–42)

- Lydia (Acts 16:14–15, 40)

- Phoebe, Mary, Junia, Tryphaena and Tryphosa, Persis, Rufus' mother, Julia, the sister of Nereus (Rom 16)

- Chloe (1 Cor 1:11)

- Euodia and Syntyche (Phil 4:2–3)

- Nympha (Col 4:15)
- Lois and Eunice (2 Tim 1:5)
- Claudia (2 Tim 4:21)
- Apphia (Phlm 1:2)
- Priscilla (Acts 18:2, 18, 26; Rom 16:3; 1 Cor 16:19)
- The mother of John Mark (Acts 12:12)
- Philip's four prophet daughters (Acts 21:9)
- The prophesying women of Corinth (1 Cor 11:2–16)[11]

The upward ministerial mobility of women appears to have continued, waning some with the institutionalization of the church as the official religion of the Roman empire but continuing beyond the formation of the formal clerical offices. For centuries after Christ, we now know that women served as deacons, priests, presbyters, and possibly even bishops, though some of the certainty of this is skewed because of the terminology used in ancient documents and variations in regional practices.[12] The continuation of this redemptive arc has taken on new life in modern times, as the Holy Spirit continues to call women to preach and to lead in the church.

THE PAULINE ARGUMENT

Despite the misogynistic reputation he gets, Paul surrounds himself with powerful women like Junia and Prisca, many of whom he lists in Rom 16. He even entrusts the delivery of the book of Romans to Phoebe, who he describes in 16:1 as a deacon.[13] So, it is clear from the accounts of both Luke in Acts and of Paul within his own letters that strong female leadership was at the cornerstone of his ministry work.

Yet, it is also clear from Scripture that there are several points in Paul's writing where he makes statements that suggest women should be silent in church (1 Cor 14:34), they should not have authority over men (1 Tim 2:12), and that men are to be the head of women (Eph 5:23; 1 Cor 11:3). It is these passages that have, for centuries, served as the justification for barring women from pastoral positions in the church—what can be called the "clobber passages." They have even served, in some contexts, to bar women

---

11. Adapted from Peppiatt, *Rediscovering Scripture's Vision for Women*, 118.

12. Madigan and Osiek, "Ordained Women in the Early Church."

13. Some translations render the term in this verse as "servant," but it is a deacon all the same.

from working outside of the home at all and the enforcement of a host of household code practices that perceive women as a functionally inferior partner to men.

So what do we make of the seemingly misogynistic passages in Paul? This is where basic hermeneutics—the process of understanding the interpretation of the biblical text—is valuable. This isn't a book on hermeneutics, so I won't get too far down the rabbit hole here, but it is crucial to consider how plucking a verse or two out of their original context can do damage to the interpretation we extrapolate from the Bible. If I simply pluck John 6:56, "Whoever eats my flesh and drinks my blood remains in me and I in them" out of the broader context of what Jesus was trying to say, I can make point to that passage and justify cannibalism or vampirism on seemingly biblical grounds! But does the Bible support cannibalism or vampirism? This would be, after all, a plain, face value reading of the text. But obviously the Bible doesn't condone cannibalism and vampirism. How do we know this? Because of the context of Jesus' words, because of the context of rest of Scripture, and from the cultural context in which those words were said.

But the same can be said of 1 Tim 2:12 where Paul says, "I do not permit a woman to teach or to assume authority over a man; she must be quiet." If I simply pluck this verse from the broader context of Paul and the rest of Scripture I can point to that case and justify patriarchy on seemingly biblical grounds. But does the Bible support patriarchy? Hardly. How do we know this? Because of the context of Paul's words, because of the context of the rest of Scripture, and from the cultural context in which those words were said.

There are a host of hermeneutic processes out there but, as a missiologist, one interpretive process I have come to greatly appreciate is Christopher Wright's "four worlds" hermeneutic. Keeping God's redemptive mission as the central theme of the whole story of Scripture, Wright notes that there are four "worlds" we must consider when approaching the text:

1. *The world behind the text*: This is the cultural context of the audiences who first received Scripture. What are the political, social, economic, customs, and more that shape their worldview and how does it differ from our own?

2. *The world of the text*: This is the literary world that informs the text. What is the genre, plot, characters, rhetorical or literary device, structure that shapes how I should approach the text? I don't read a recipe the same way I read a novel (although those stories that precede recipes online can *be* novels!) so I shouldn't read biblical poetry the same way I read narratives or letters.

3. *The world above the text*: This is what I call a "biblical worldview." That is, attempting to see what's happening through the lens of God's divine perspective. How does this text fit within the overarching story of the mission of God to redeem all of creation in Jesus the Christ?

4. *The world in front of the text*: This is our world. What assumptions am I bringing to the text from my own culture, race, education, political viewpoints, etc. How can the principles I've observed in the biblical text inform my own way of living on mission with God today in my context?[14]

This, as well as any other faithful reading of Scripture, causes us to back away from removing a verse from its context to throw it up as a prooftext for whatever argument we wish to win, behavior we wish to regulate, or opinion we wish to codify as biblical truth. Instead, it calls us to see Paul, and the rest of the Bible, as a unified and cohesive whole. When we look at Paul's words in the seemingly patriarchal texts, we should do so set within the broader perspective of Scripture. In doing this, we see that there are specific situations Paul is addressing in the churches of Ephesus and Corinth. As he is addressing them in one hand, his ministry is elevating the status of women with the other. And when we stop to recognize that the emphases *we* read into the text such as "wives, submit to your husbands" are not the lines that Paul's ancient readers would have emphasized, such as "husbands, love your wives as Christ loves the church." I will return to Paul's clobber passages more in chapter six, but for now, we must work to return Paul's words back within their original context and consider that a face-value reading in these instances may not be the most faithful reading of the text.

THE CROSS-CULTURAL ARGUMENT

Anyone that believes they can approach the Bible completely objectively is only fooling themselves. We bring our subjectivity, opinions, and worldview to the text in ways that we are often completely unaware of. The ways we see the world, such as our perception of time, family, relationships, economics, and more, unconsciously impose themselves onto the biblical text when we read it. We naturally read our worldview into the biblical text. The problem is that the people who first received and read the Bible had a wildly different worldview than we do.

This doesn't mean we cannot properly understand Scripture, but it does mean that the two thousand years of history, differences of language,

14. Wright, *Truth with a Mission*.

culture, and geographic situation requires that we try to mitigate imposing our worldview onto the Bible as much as we can, like a surgeon who scrubs in for surgery before performing that surgery. We do this by learning about and seeking to understand other cultures—especially those cultures most similar to the cultures of the Bible.[15]

One such cultural difference between "their" culture and "ours" (those two categories are *big* brushes with which to paint!) is in the relationship between rules and relationships. In the modern West, rules govern relationships. We conform our relationships to rules, and those rules are applicable to everyone within a certain group of people[16] (e.g., an employee handbook for a company or HOA regulations for a community). I like to describe rules to Western relationships like a planter pot for a houseplant: the pot (i.e., the rules) gives space for the plant (i.e., the relationships) to live and breathe but also constrains the plant from growing beyond what it is supposed to.

But in the ancient world, it was the relationships that governed rules. By this I mean, that rules and relationships were more like a trellis and a tomato plant. A trellis (i.e., the rules) gives structure to support the growth of the plant (i.e., the relationships), but the trellis does not restrict its growth. This means that, for the cultures of the Bible, rules were applicable—*until they weren't*. In our culture, giving exception to rules for certain people or circumstances is frowned upon. It's unfair at best, hypocritical at worse. But for the ancients, rules were only good insofar as they contributed to the harmony and flourishing of human relationships. So, to give exception to them was not hypocrisy; it was valuing relationship.[17]

What does this have to do with women? As I've argued until now, Scripture paints for us a picture of the full empowerment of women in society and in the church. However, even if I was wrong, and all of what I've written in this chapter up until now is mistaken, and the apostles did forbid women from serving as pastors, there would still be exceptions to the rules.

If that were the case, the New Testament church would have *at best* considered that a rule that was applicable *until it wasn't*. Take Richards and O'Brien's experience at a pastors' conference for example:

> While I (Randy) was living in Indonesia, I was invited to speak
> at a "pastors only" meeting. In the audience of over one hundred

---

15. For more, see Georges, *3D Gospel*; Georges, *Ministering in Patronage Cultures*; Richards and O'Brien, *Misreading Scripture with Western Eyes*; Richards and James, *Misreading Scripture with Individualist Eyes*.

16. Richards and O'Brien, *Misreading Scripture with Western Eyes*, 169.

17. Richards and O'Brien, *Misreading Scripture with Western Eyes*, 169.

> pastors, I noticed a half-dozen women. The bylaws of the Convention of Indonesian Baptist Churches clearly state: "Pastors must be male." I should have left it alone.
>
> "I thought this meeting was for pastors only," I remarked to the conference organizer.
>
> "It is," he replied.
>
> "But there were women in the audience," I pointed out.
>
> "Yes."
>
> Now I was confused. "But your laws say pastors must be male!" I exclaimed.
>
> The convention president calmly replied, "Yes, and most of them are."
>
> Goodness. His answer represents a fundamentally different view of law . To the non-Western mind, it seems, a law is more a guideline. Americans would likely want to change the Indonesian law to read, "Most pastors must be male," and then we would argue over the percentage. The Indonesian—and arguably the biblical—view of law always left room for exceptions.
>
> Paul states, "I do not permit a woman to teach or to assume authority over a man; she must be quiet" (1 Tim. 2:12). "But what about Priscilla and Junia?" we might ask Paul. "They taught in church. You said women must keep silent."
>
> Perhaps Paul would answer, "Yes. And most of them do."[18]

Situational rules like this are difficult for us to wrap our minds around here in the West, as the excerpt notes. But what we see in this example of Indonesian Baptists is the same sort of dispensing of rules to give priority to the harmony and flourishing of the community that would have been the cultural norm for Paul and his churches. The needs of the context mattered more than the universal application of rules because the chief concern was for the *shalom* of the Christian community, not the enforcement of arbitrary rules for their own sake.

But, if this were the case, we might then wonder what conclusions Paul would reach about applying gender-based prohibitions in our churches in the West today. Paul's two chief concerns as he discipled his churches appears from Scripture to be: 1) the unity of the local church community and (related) 2) the gospel witness of that church community to the surrounding culture. While I can't speak for Paul, I do believe that prohibiting women from living as functional equals, in both status and role, has a profoundly

---

18. Richards and O'Brien, *Misreading Scripture with Western Eyes*, 169–70.

negative impact on both church unity and gospel witness. As these were chief concerns for Paul, I believe he would most certainly rebuke our enforcement of gender-based prohibitions at the expense of our gospel witness.

Chapter 3

The Diversity of the Female Calling

I've found that sometimes I don't listen well. And while I know a lot of other men that can identify with that sentiment as well, I can only speak for myself. I've often struggled to listen—not simply hear but *listen*. There's a bit of a difference between hearing and listening. Hearing is when your brain receives the words of another person. Listening is when your brain receives the words of another person and promptly delivers those words to your heart.

I've found that when I only hear but do not listen, my internal filter takes over and I begin to (in real time) filter the words someone is speaking to me through my cerebral sorting machine until I can neatly categorize the data into something with which I'm familiar. While I cannot be completely certain, I assume I'm not alone in that practice.

While I've improved in my capacity to listen in more recent years, Tara had to suffer through our newlywed years with my penchant for not listening. Couple that reality with the fact that I was an arrogant twenty-two-year-old who thought I knew everything there was to know about any subject, and I was a real peach when it came to communication.

I struggled with communicating well in our early years of marriage, even leading up to when we planted our church in Flint, Michigan, almost ten years ago and began the difficult practice of co-pastoring together. When Tara would share with me about her calling and what she felt like God was doing in and through her vocationally, I put my *hearing* into practice, but I didn't listen. I filtered her words through my brain, but it took a frustrating degree of repetition on Tara's part before I understood it with my heart.

I therefore made assumptions about Tara's call. While I knew she felt called to be a pastor, there were complexities about her calling that didn't fit neatly into my cerebral sorting machine. So, rather than listening for the nuances, I simply chose to hear my assumptions.

The longer we were in the pastorate as well as just "adulting" (as we millennials love to call it), the more I encountered women who felt a calling to pastor but not always the same way Tara did. Some were completely content and felt they flourished best in a ministry support or administrative role. Others wanted to travel and preach itinerantly. Still other women expressed a calling to support their husband who was a pastor but did not feel that vocational calling themselves. Their ministry was in the marketplace. Other women I've known feel called to be stay-at-home mothers—something in my early years I figured most women would want to be freed from in favor of working in the marketplace or in church life.

What I began to realize is that the female calling is, quite literally, as diverse as there are females! That's because God's call upon a woman's life is not a one-size-fits all solution. This was difficult for my twenty-something mind to grasp when I associated the idea of a strong woman with a particular variety of personality attributes, leadership practices, and even vocational positions. But I've learned that to understand a woman's calling requires first that one seeks to understand the woman. While not an exhaustive list by any means, here are a few examples of leadership types I've observed among women and a patroness saint of sorts, for each, to characterize them.

THE DEBORAH

The book of Judges describes Deborah as *the* leader. In the Hebrew story, before the united monarchy established under the reign of King Saul, the twelve tribes of Israel were governed by a series of judges, which was a sort of political and military leader. Deborah was one such judge.

A Deborah kind of leader is the woman who feels a calling to be "the one." Whether it is the senior pastor of a church, the head of a business, the director of a non-profit, a Deborah is an executive level leader. She calls the shots and she drives forward whatever it is that she leads.

Women who are Deborah leaders are frequently criticized for being domineering and controlling. Many men struggle to be led by Deborahs because their capacity to lead (often better than the men around them) threatens the sensitive male ego. Deborah leaders may feel as though they need to tow a fine line between what is perceived as "masculine" and "feminine." They feel they have to take charge as men are stereotypically thought to do but have to show extra niceness to avoid being labeled as a [insert derogatory term *du jour*]. They're likely the type of woman who feels the pressure to add exclamation points and emojis to emails to avoid coming across too sternly. As has often been the case in American politics and media, Deborah leaders will even work to lower the pitch of their speaking voice to be taken more seriously.

THE PHOEBE

Phoebe was clearly indispensable to Paul's ministry but as a deaconess was not "the one." She was "the one's one." Phoebe was that strong supporting role that is indispensable to the show. When I think of outstanding Phoebes I think of women like the acclaimed actress Kathy Bates. Bates has had lead roles in various works (the most well-known of which is likely a toss between Annie Wilkes in *Misery* or Evelyn Couch in *Fried Green Tomatoes*), but the work I love most of hers are those times where she gets to play the supporting actress who makes all the difference in the plotline. What would *The Waterboy* be without Mama? *The Office's* Sabre plotline without its CEO Jo Bennett? Would *Titanic* even be worth watching today if Bates hadn't played socialite Molly Brown? Bates' presence in any number of small or big screen performances illustrates the power of a dynamic Phoebe leader. And, within American culture in particular, it is quite special to find someone who feels uniquely gifted to sit in the second chair.

I've observed that Phoebes often struggle to feel understood. Phoebes frequently possess the same leadership skills and acumen of the Deborahs they serve, so people often assume Phoebes are simply Deborahs-in-waiting. In other situations, the mixture of their leadership capability and their gender may get them pigeonholed in administrative roles for which they are overqualified. I've observed that a combination of a close and competent Deborah and Phoebe in any organization is quite a sight to behold. You want to see stuff get done? Put a strong female leader in both the number one and number two spots in an organization. Stuff will get done.

However, the reality is that more Phoebes work for "Dons" than Deborahs. So, while I'll address barriers for women in a later chapter, one of the biggest barriers faced by Phoebes are the men with whom they work. In church settings, accountability practices like the Billy Graham Rule often prohibit Phoebes from flourishing in their roles (or even getting the role in the first place). The presence of a Phoebe is sometimes difficult for men in work environments when they have been conditioned to view all encounters with the women through a sexualized lens (even if that sexualized lens is an avoidant one). Phoebes often brush up against glass ceilings or unspoken cultural practices within an organization because of where in an organizational chart their feminine giftings are placed.

THE MARTHA

Martha gets a bad reputation for her being about the business of the little dinner party where Jesus commends Mary's choice to sit and learn in Luke 10. But while Mary is praised for her breach of culturally-defined protocol (the learning stuff was only for the menfolk in those days), Martha was doing what women were expected to do—administrate the event.

Indeed, many women come alive when they are empowered to function in an administrative capacity. Whether it is leading at an administrative level or being an administrative assistant, for many women this is a calling from God and one for which they have been uniquely gifted. Marthas are what keep organizations moving. They are the ones that do so much of the behind the scenes work that is often taken for granted when people show up to an event, conference, church service, etc. Yet, without them, the lives of other types tend to fall apart.

I have a special place in my heart for Marthas, primarily because I lack administrative skill myself. Administratively-inclined people—especially those for whom it is a calling, are a true gift to the world. Their "behind-the-scenes" nature is only undervalued in spaces where platform and power reign supreme. In the upside-down way of the kingdom, it is these often-unsung vocations like the Martha that are treasured most, precisely because their reward is seldom in earthly applause. But great is their reward in the age to come.

THE LYDIA

I mentioned Lydia before—the first recorded European convert to Christianity. A wealthy cloth merchant, Lydia opened her home to the Paul and his companions and housed the first church in Philippi in her home. A Lydia-type calling is one that is graced with the vocation of hospitality.

Hospitality is something of a lost art in American culture. We tend to view the home as a refuge *away* from people rather than a place to receive people. This is demonstrated in no greater way perhaps than in the way houses are now built. When our family lived in Michigan, we lived in a home that was built in 1929. It was *made* for receiving guests. A giant front porch was the feature of the front of the house, while a detached garage was situated in the back of the property. As such, we had to drive behind our house to park our car. Inevitably, as with many urban lots, the short trek from the garage to the back entrance to the house involved small talk with my neighbor, whose home was similarly constructed. The home had a formal dining room which we frequently employed to welcome friends and family—especially on our annual church cookout to celebrate Pentecost Sunday.

But we've also lived in two newly-built homes since we were first married. While we loved both of those new homes, there was virtually no front porch to speak of on either new house. The front porch on many new houses is replaced as the feature point of the front of a home by a protruding, attached garage, allowing a homeowner the ability to zoom his or her car right into the garage and close it without ever having to see the neighbors. We still entertained guests in those houses, but they weren't as conducive to that entertainment as that old house with the giant front porch, beckoning neighbors to visit. Architecture communicates value, and we don't really value hospitality like we once did.

Enter the Lydia.

Lydias are the keepers of the soul of hospitality that is dying out in American culture. I'm not just talking about someone who knows how to throw a good soirée. A Lydia is a woman who views her ability to entertain, to make people feel welcomed and beloved, and to walk away with a memorable experience as her birthright. It is what she is built for. They view hospitality as more than just meeting culturally-imposed expectations for etiquette. It is, for them, a spiritual experience—an act of worship to God. Through her hospitality, a Lydia reflects the excellence of God to her guests and attunes her guests to the loving and all-embracing God she represents.

To have a Lydia in your life is to have a good thing. But like the Martha, they are often overlooked for just how deeply spiritual and vocational such a calling to hospitality truly is. They might simply be regarded as the woman who knows how to throw a good party or who always makes people feel welcomed. However, Lydias are, in many ways, the leaders of the church of the future which will become increasingly dependent upon her skills as the current trend of program- and platform-centered church life is on the way out. Whether her paying job is in the marketplace or in the church, Lydias will be a crucial pastoral type in the church of tomorrow for it to thrive in the years to come.

THE PRISCILLA

Priscilla (also known as Prisca) ministered with Paul alongside her husband Aquila. It is interesting to note that when Scripture mentions this pair, it is Priscilla who is mentioned before her husband. Again, the order in which things are listed in the Bible is significant, and Priscilla's mention before Aquila has led many to suggest that she held a role of greater significance than that of her husband, or that Luke intentionally inverts their names from the normal order to emphasize their co-pastoral function in ministry.

Whatever the case, Acts 18:24–28 describes how Priscilla, alongside Aquila, received Apollos "into their circle of friends" (18:26) and instructed him in the way of the Lord. Priscilla possessed a capacity to teach and disciple the way of Jesus to such an extent that even Apollos, who is described as being well-educated and effective (18:24) and who accurately taught the way of Jesus (18:25), benefitted from her instruction. What's more, the ministry of Priscilla also likely included a stay (how long, we do not know) in Ephesus to teach in the synagogue, which was open to the teaching of Jesus.[1]

Priscillas are women with the calling to instruction. This may include public teaching, such as the clear gift of Beth Moore today in her capacity to bring to life the pages of Scripture in a way that has been impactful to scores of individuals (including myself). For others, the Priscilla gift may take the form of a more private instruction—that is, mentorship and discipleship. Some women possess the calling for both.

What I have observed about the Priscilla is how she is often criticized when her giftings and calling bring her into public instruction and are overlooked when it is done privately. The Priscilla is a difficult vocation to take up, yet she is most crucial for the benefit of the body of Christ. Priscillas are often viewed as stepping outside of the bounds of the role for their gender when they instruct publicly, citing Paul's words in 1 Cor 14:34 that women should be silent in the assembly. Ironically, this logic fails to reconcile to recognize that Paul's discourse about head coverings in chapter 11 is in reference to when women "pray or prophesy" (11:4). And, given the surrounding context about the Corinthians' shared life together as the church, Paul is most certainly speaking about women leading prayer and prophesy in their worship gatherings.[2] So while they're often criticized for instructing in churches, the Spirit calls Priscillas to do just that.

Our churches are chock-full of women who do the quiet work of discipleship, often when men have abandoned the pursuit in favor of more

---

1. Keener, *IVP Bible Background Commentary*, 377.
2. Keener, *IVP Bible Background Commentary*, 476.

glamorous endeavors on the platform. Priscillas are mentoring over the phone, over coffee, at playgrounds, on social media, and more. They're the unsung heroines who are raising up the next generation in the faith so that it endures. That is not to discount the very real presence of Aquilas in the church as well—men who are about the task of instruction, both publicly and privately. But one thing is for certain, Christian community flourishes best when it empowers both Aquilas *and* Priscillas to carry out their God-given vocation of instruction.

THE ESTHER

Esther is memorable to us because of her willingness to speak truth to power. The book of Esther describes a woman of low social standing, who was taken without consent and made the wife of the king. The chasm of power between Esther and the king is almost unfathomable to those of us in a modern democracy. Esther's action to speak truth to power on behalf of her people is a significant prophetic act. Thus, the Esther is the prophetic vocation of womanhood.

The term "prophetic" can have multiple implications, usually dependent upon what Christian tradition is using the term. Being Pentecostal, the term prophetic is often connected to *fore*telling that something will happen, either by God's design or allowance. Other traditions often speak of the prophetic as a *forth*telling act—speaking truth to power to see God's design for people come to fruition (as we see in Esther). What's more, there is a dynamic to prophesy that is incarnational as well—living God's design for humankind so that our lives are a prophetic foretaste of the kingdom.[3]

In some respects, the prophetic office is all three of these playing in sync with one another—a times one characteristic plays melody while the others play harmony, and then it may change based on the leading of the Holy Spirit. Without these prophetic characteristics playing in sync, each is prone toward its own particular excess. A foretelling-heavy Esther is often the type that gives the prophetic a bad name. Whether it be on Christian television or some YouTube channel, there is no shortage of foretelling-heavy prophesy, often forecasting doom and gloom (and peddling something in the process). A forthtelling-heavy Esther can easily be coopted by the social justice issues of the day—not speaking into them as a mouthpiece of the Spirit, but having her voice hijacked by the issue without the nuance of Spirit-given perspective. Finally, an incarnation-heavy Esther may *live*

---

3. Hoekendijk, *Church Inside Out*, 25; Rohr, *Eager to Love*, 41–43.

that prophetic reality, but lacks the gumption to speak about it when it matters most.

Like the prophetic office in general, the call of an Esther can be a painful one. Esthers give people—often people in positions of power—news they don't want to hear. They expose idols. Their words attempt to shift the streams of power toward the marginalized and oppressed and away from those who control the water spigot. Thus, a prophetic vocation in general can be a lonely one—but an Esther, a prophetic *woman*, can be especially lonely and misunderstood.

THE MARY

Mary's choices in Luke 10, to forego the cultural duties assigned to women for hosting guests and instead sit and learn from Jesus was quite a remarkable breach of etiquette. There was no reason for women to learn, because women belonged in spaces for which learning was largely unnecessary. But Mary chose to stay with the men and to learn at the feet of the Rabbi, much to the dismay of Martha (and others). Martha's rebuke of Mary to Jesus was a culturally-appropriate attempt to shame Mary into falling back into line. But Jesus would hear none of it. He lauded Mary for her choice to sit, listen, and learn.

The Marys of womanhood are the lifelong learners. Marys are perpetual students, regardless of their position. They're hungry for knowledge in general, and knowledge of the things of God in particular. They crave to not simply know more *about* God, but that their knowledge would aid them in their pursuit of knowing God more. Marys take seriously Jesus' words in Matthew 22:37 when he says the greatest commandment is to love the Lord with, among other things, all of one's mind.

While learned women are abundant in the marketplace and other forms of non-ecclesial leadership, women who desire to be life-long learners of Scripture and theology are often met with the same underlying misunderstanding that Mary herself experienced: why learn about theology and ministry when you can't be a pastor? I witnessed this on Twitter several weeks before typing these words, where a woman received a degree in pastoral ministry only for the curmudgeon corners of the Christian Twittersphere to explode with handwringing over the news.

Besides the obvious issue with asserting women cannot be pastors (which we've already addressed in a previous chapter), the insistence that Marys should not or cannot pursue a field of theological study (formally or informally) because of supposed gender-based restrictions on what she might do with it is a woeful departure from the doctrine of the priesthood of all believers. The priesthood of all believers emerged from the Reformation to recover the agile mobilization of the New Testament church. It asserted that every Christian, regardless of whether they were clergy, was entrusted with a priestly function to carry out in life.

For Protestants, this doctrine is at the very foundation of what we've believed for the last five hundred years, yet some would suggest that Marys should be restricted in how they walk that out based solely upon their gender. In turn, Marys often face opposition when their hunger to learn crosses into the taboo waters of such topics as pastoral theology. When an outright hostility is not a feature, Marys often experience a bewilderment at best for wanting to venture into the theological end of the learning pool.

But Marys are crucial to the health of the church's collective theological responsibility. It is through their voice, their unique insight into the Scripture, and their perspective of church life, that we move beyond a theological landscape that has, for centuries, been dominated by white men. We need Marys of all varieties—learning Marys with formal degrees and learning Marys with simply the hunger to know their God more and bless the rest of us with their insight.

There are likely a hundred more variations to the diverse expressions of the female calling. My list is only to meant to illustrate a few of those that I have observed most frequently and to provide some observational insight as to how they function within Christian community and to also highlight some of their challenges.

When Tara read through these types of callings she made an important observation that, rather than taking her insight and passing it off as my own (as we men have a horrible habit of doing to our female counterparts), I felt important to share verbatim:

> The most complex thing about God's calling on women's lives is that it most often encompasses not just one of these characteristics, but a few. It can vacillate between one or another based on the environment the woman is in. It happens nearly seamlessly, which also hinders men from understanding women's calling.

She's right. And I confess that I've had the besetting habit of not recognizing when Tara's own calling "type" has shifted. Not unlike popular personality insights like the Enneagram, where one has a dominant type with a secondary wing, so too women may possess more than one of these calling types simultaneously, and they may change over the course of time, as God develops them as a leader, as outside circumstances change requiring that women adapt in order to survive, and as they mature in their own sense of who they are as a beloved daughter in Christ.

BIBLICAL MANHOOD'S RESPONSE

But the inevitable question is "so what?" It's one thing to recognize a calling in a woman. But for those of us who have women in our lives who we desire to support and empower—how do we do that? I've found that in my efforts to support Tara in her calling, I have often accidentally become a roadblock because of my posture of hearing instead of listening. I place assumptions on her about what I think her calling is, when it is quite something different altogether. At present, I will address several ways men can support the women in their lives as they walk out God's unique calling over them.

Listen

"Listen" is such a simple word, but if most men are honest, we often struggle to listen instead of hear. As our minds receive information we instinctively leap into diagnostic mode, attempting to identify the problem and think through a solution. Often we have a solution in mind before the person speaking to us has even finished describing the problem!

But listening well is a characteristic modeled to us by the men of all men—Jesus. Jesus had what Randy Reese and Robert Loane refer to as a "particularizing way with others."[4] He uniquely noticed people. We can reasonably assume that he didn't look past people, scanning the crowd for a more important person to talk to. He observed an open posture where he was touched by the lives of those who approached him. Henri Nouwen describes the challenges for creating this sort of open posture in our lives:

> Someone who is filled with ideas, concepts, opinions, and convictions cannot be a good host. There is no inner space to listen, no openness to discover the gift of the other. It is not difficult to see how those "who know it all" can kill a conversation and prevent an interchange of ideas. Poverty of mind as a spiritual attitude is a growing willingness to recognize the incomprehensibility of the mystery of life. The more mature we become the more we will be able to give up our inclination to grasp, catch,

---

4. Reese and Loane, *Deep Mentoring*, 182–84.

and comprehend the fullness of life and the more we will be ready to let life enter into us.[5]

Nouwen illuminates an important concept when he speaks of the "poverty of the mind." This is not a lack of intelligence, wisdom, or wit that we often think about when we hear a phrase like that. Instead, it's a freedom to not be right, not be heard, not win an argument, or not prove the other person wrong. It is even a freedom from the need to understand. Instead, it is a critical openness to create a listening space where the other person can be heard and we can be impacted by their perspective. By *critical* openness, I mean that this listening posture does not mean we are always convinced, but rather we hold a tension where we can "agree to disagree" and both parties feel heard, seen, and loved.

Empowering the calling of women begins first by a posture of open listening. Not rushing to solutions or quick fixes. But genuinely listening and responding accordingly. Men will find that as they observe this posture with their wives, it even enhances the fruitfulness of their marriage relationship. The desire to feel seen and understood isn't unique to women, but it would do us men very well to pay careful attention to our posture of listening toward the women in our lives, especially as it pertains to how they perceive God doing in work in them.

Don't Impose

Next, we should avoid imposing our assumptions on women as to what we believe their calling is or should be. This of course includes the subset of Christianity that insist that a woman's place is not in the board room or the pulpit, but it's not just a principle for them. It's a principle to be heeded cautiously by those like myself who believe that women can serve and flourish wherever God calls them, and because of the victory of Christ, their gender places no restriction upon them. I confess that where I have struggled in the past is recognizing that egalitarian living means that God's design is that women can serve in all areas of church and marketplace—but also that they are free *not* to.

The egalitarian view is that women are free in Christ to flourish in the unique calling God has placed on their lives, even if it doesn't fit the mold we prefer or assume. By refusing to impose our assumptions on women, we refrain from telling women they can't be pastors or CEOs but also refrain from telling them they *must* be. Some women feel deeply called by God to

---

5. Nouwen, *Reaching Out*, 74.

be stay-at-home moms. Some feel that they've been designed by God to focus solely on raising God-loving children. Some feel that they flourish best when they work in support roles. Inasmuch as we would do well to not impose our opinions about what women cannot do with their calling, we would do equally well to avoid imposing our opinions about what they must do.

Expect Change

While we assume that all people change to some extent over time, we are often more prone to recognizing the evolution of our own calling than in someone else. While there are timeless characteristics about who God has uniquely fashioned each of his beloved daughters and sons to be, that does not mean that how that uniqueness is walked out in life and vocation won't change or evolve over time. In particular, when people walk through traumatic experiences or other seismic shifts in their lives—the death of a loved one, a crisis of identity, a dark night of the soul—this has profound impact on an individual's worldview, and therefore also their sense of placement in the world around them.[6]

It's reasonable to expect that the women in our lives will grow and change over time. It's reasonable to expect that the hardships and breakthroughs brought upon them in life will also impact their sense of identity and calling. God uses the sovereign foundations he builds in a woman early in her life to prepare her for more fruitful years later on. This likely means that those foundational years will look different than the latter years, just as the frame of a house is noticeably different than the foundation that supports it.

We should expect the sense of calling in the women in our lives to adapt and change as they grow and change. Our supportive task is to continue in a posture of receptive listening as they walk through that evolution. The difficulty I have found as I have walked through this with Tara and other women with whom we are acquainted is that there is a delicate rhythm to which one must attend. I must be engaged enough with someone undergoing these sorts of change seasons as to ask probing questions, help her to think critically and as objectively as possible about what she's walking through, and be that sort of spiritual friend that can aid in attuning her to the voice of the Holy Spirit—all of this without trying to import my assumptions, come off as critical of the change, or to assume the role of the Holy Spirit himself.

I don't believe this is possible to do perfectly. That's not the point. Our broken humanity limits our capacity to do much of anything with

6. Hiebert, *Transforming Worldviews*, 317–18.

perfection. But it's not about abiding *perfectly* but abiding *faithfully* with the women in our lives as they seek out God's unique design for them that makes all the difference.

Advocate

As I've said earlier, moving being a passive support for the calling of women into a passionate advocacy is *le besoin de l'heure*—the need of the hour. Within churches, non-profit organizations, businesses, community groups, etc., there is an imminent need for people—and men, in particular—who are willing to advocate for the God-given right for women to walk out the calling God has placed upon them. There is a particular sort of privilege that patriarchy affords to men, even in spaces that we would call egalitarian. This privilege allows men to speak up where women often feel required to be silent. It allows us to be a bit of a bulldog where women fear they will come off as too feminist. It permits us the ability to demand equity in situations where women may be concerned that making such a demand might be perceived as self-serving.

There is a special kind of biblical manhood that the Bible calls us to embrace. Indeed, it is a more *biblical* variety of biblical manhood than some who use that term to prop up a 1950s *Leave it to Beaver* version of American manhood.

It is a biblical manhood that walks in the way of Jesus—a Jesus who spoke up for women (Luke 7:36–50).

It's a biblical manhood that goes out of the way to elevate the status of women in their community (John 4:1–26).

It's a biblical manhood that fights for a woman's right to sit in spaces normally reserved for men (Luke 10:38–42).

This variety of biblical manhood doesn't need to adorn itself in camouflage and play with swords and use military imagery and participate in axe-throwing competitions and all of the other culturally-specific perspectives of how a "real man" should be. Instead, it is confident enough in its own place in God's kingdom as to take up the noble cause of elevating the voice of women instead of silencing it. *Biblical* biblical manhood doesn't engage in the make-believe fantasy that men are knights rescuing fair damsels locked inside the castle of feminism. Instead, it takes up the mantle of slaying the fire-breathing dragon of patriarchy so that women may walk out the calling God has placed upon their lives.

If you want a noble, manly task to take up, advocate for women.

Sacrifice

We all have our own career ambitions. We have goals we hope to meet. And, if we men are honest about our own marriages—many of us are fine with our wives shining bright, so long as they don't outshine us. Our egos have a nasty way of getting in the way sometimes. I must admit that this was the case for me early in my marriage. I genuinely wanted Tara to succeed—but if I were truly honest with myself, it was only so long as I was succeeding just a little *more*. I wanted her to run into the wide-open spaces of the calling God had placed upon her—so long as I was just a few feet ahead in mine.

I confess that is hard to admit. But it's the truth. And I know I'm not alone in that. Few might explicitly admit it. But the symptoms of it are there. And if so many of us have this dark side in our souls that can cause us to feel insecure and even threatened by the calling of our *wife*, how much more do we unconsciously perceive women we work with as potential threats to our own success?

The antidote to this is to sacrifice. The cure to our paranoia of position and idolatry of opportunity and success is to *give it away*. Are you and a woman both up for a promotion and you know deep down inside that she'd be a better fit? Bow out. Pastors, if you have a preaching opportunity—give it to away to a woman. If you're sitting in a meeting and you have the chance to take credit for something you worked on with a woman on your team—heap the praise onto her.

Advocacy necessarily involves sacrifice. And sacrifice, by definition, hurts. But several years ago, I began moving into a posture of sacrifice in my advocacy toward women in church ministry. What I found is that it has a way of coming back around to bless you. Opportunity is a limited resource, but it is not a non-renewable resource. And hear me: women around you notice when you give opportunity away to women (they also see when you hoard it like a squirrel preparing for winter). They see when you have set aside your own ambitions temporarily for their sake. They take note.

One example from my own life was with a young woman (we'll call her Anne) who was in an entry-level position on the staff of a megachurch at which we once worked. When I joined the staff, I was in charge of directing the production of a lot of the discipleship resources our church produced for the congregation. At one point, I enlisted Anne's help to prepare a devotional, and I was absolutely floored by the quality of her writing and biblical insight. It was simply tremendous work.

After the resource was produced, I was in a meeting with the rest of the church's senior team and the resource was brought up. People in the meeting talked about how wonderful it was and thanked *me* for putting it together. Anne wasn't in the room. In that moment, I had the opportunity to take credit. In this particular staff culture it would have benefitted me much more to take credit in the meeting than to pass it on to Anne. No one would have thought anything of it. But I chose instead to redirect the praise onto Anne. I talked about how she had really done the heavy lifting and what a gifted writer she was and how, even though she wasn't on my team, I would like her to be placed on my team if the opportunity ever arose. A couple years of later, I had another opportunity to advocate for Anne and some female staff who were being overlooked by a senior leader. Fast forward again to when I announced that I was writing *Your Daughters Shall Prophesy*, Anne was one of the first to reach out and offer her assistance in getting the word out about the book.

I don't share this story to pat myself on the back. Believe me, there have been plenty of times where I got it wrong in the advocacy department. But I share it with the hopes that it will illustrate just how the simple opportunities that arise to sacrifice praise, pass up opportunity, or redistribute power have a sowing and reaping effect on our lives. That shouldn't be the motivation for our advocacy and sacrifice, but it should serve to dispel unspoken concerns that such sacrifice will irreparably damage our own careers. I've found it to have quite the opposite result, in fact.

CHAPTER 4

Power Ain't Pie

I'M NOT REALLY A dessert guy. If I'm going to blow my daily caloric intake out of the water, I'd rather do it by eating any number of deep fried or cheese-drenched delicacies. Give me stromboli over a cupcake any day. *Except* as it pertains to pie—pecan pie in particular. Whether one pronounces it *pe-CAHN*, *pEE-cahn*, or *pEE-can* makes no difference to me so long as a big piece of it is topped with some French vanilla ice cream and it finds its way onto my plate. And while I'm a fairly generous person, that all goes out the window when it comes down to a food I love, like pecan pie. I cease to be a pastor—visibly cease to be discernably Christian, perhaps! In those moments I'm nothing more than a starved (and slightly deranged) German Shepherd guarding a ham hock against the rest of the pack.

While that might be a bit hyperbolic, I would be lying if I said that, when faced with a pecan pie and the social expectation of sharing that pie with others, there wasn't some degree of internalized temptation to grab the pie and head for the hills before anyone else can get their grubby mitts on it. Why? Because in any situation pie is a scarce resource—especially pecan pie! After all, when was the last time you were at a social gathering where they had all-you-can-eat pecan pie? It just doesn't happen.

So, if you get some of the pie, that means I get less. That's how limited and scarce resources work. If there's more for you, there's inevitably less for me. And when I'm hungry to satisfy my pecan pie craving, the temptation is very real to find subtle, socially-acceptable ways for me to sneak just a little bit more.

That's how many people view power in organizational and social settings. If I have less power, then someone inevitably has more, and this can put my status, control, or (depending on the situation) safety in jeopardy. If I have more, than you have less, which is a safer and more secure place to be. People often view power like they view pie.

Wilmer Villacorta, assistant professor of intercultural studies at Fuller Theological Seminary, says that there is a "correlation between the human condition and the human sense of power" and that it "has to do with the innate desire to prove our worthiness." He goes on to add,

> Since humanity has lost its sense of closeness with God, the human soul hungers and thirsts for approval and meaning. Ultimately the quest for this sense of worthiness compels the human soul to seek power instead of the source of true happiness.[1]

Villacorta drills down into the human impetus for power: significance and meaning. Having worked in turbulent and dysfunctional organizations myself, I would add that there is also an element of psychological and social safety wrapped up in the quest for power as well. The human pursuit of power is fundamentally a quest for safety and significance. If I have power, I have control. And if I have control, then I inevitably have the capacity to have some degree of say over my destiny and the destiny of others. I have some capacity to influence the outcome of the people group to whom I belong and, in return, receive the due praise for being one of such great influence.

The trouble, as I will show in this chapter, is that power is *not* a limited resource. And when we treat it as such, dysfunction, oppression, and abuse inevitably follow. History has shown that when power is stewarded as something to be hoarded, to be gathered for one's own benefit, or so that one or a few may have the final say in determining the destiny of the masses, the most vulnerable of a society are more acutely impacted. History has also shown us that most often the most vulnerable in a society include the disabled, the infirm, the poor, children, and *women*.

One need only pick any number of examples from military history to see a repeated pattern: powerful men send men without power off to fight one another to enhance the status and condition of the powerful men. The worst burdens of those power struggles are always disproportionately heaped upon those who are most vulnerable, including women.

Even when military conflict is not at hand, women still most often and most acutely find themselves on the ugly end of the wars over power.

---

1. Villacorta. *Tug of War*, 36.

On the battlefield or in the board room, women feel the sting of the self-ish stewardship of power most acutely. It can be something as simple as an important event held by a church where male staff make the decision to assign all female staff to serve in the nursery, quenching the feminine voice in the event. It may be an organization in which men in power reorganize the organizational structure without female input, and women find themselves lower on the hierarchal totem pole. It may be a business where men are tasked with determining healthcare standard operating procedures or insurance coverage and, without female input, make determinations that adversely impact the lives of working mothers.

This is all the fruit of treating power like I treat pie—a limited resource to be gathered and hoarded and guarded so that I might have more so that you will inevitably have less. At present we will discuss power as a limited resource and as an unlimited resource, and I will offer a vision for stewarding power in the way of Jesus.

POWER AS A LIMITED RESOURCE: BABEL POWER[2]

To steward power as a limited resource is to steward power in the way of Babel. We find the story of Babel in Gen 11, where power brokers among the people (the Bible doesn't say who) determined, "let's build *for ourselves* a city and a tower with its top in the sky, and *let's make a name for ourselves* so that we won't be dispersed over all the earth" (11:4, emphasis added). What we see at play here are the two motivations of limited power that I mentioned earlier: significance and security.

First, what's essentially being described in Gen 11 is the establishment of one of humanity's first urban centers. At the center of that city, they suggest to build an ancient pagan temple called a ziggurat. Ziggurats were ancient temple complexes that provided intersections between heaven and earth, where the priestly class could beckon Babel's gods to descend and confer blessings. They weren't building a precursor to the Jerusalem temple. It was a temple to establish a connection with (and solicit power from) other gods.[3] In doing so, the people (specifically those making the decisions on behalf of the people) could establish a significance and authority for

---

2. For a more extensive treatment of the relationship between the Babel story and power, see Lamm, "Why Read The Bible In Hebrew?"

3. Walton et al., *IVP Bible Background Commentary*, 42; Heiser, *Unseen Realm*, 114–115.

themselves (Heb. *shem* or "name"). Once they had a name for themselves, they no longer would have any need for YHWH.

It is interesting to note that "mak[ing] a name" (Gen 11:4) is not necessarily a bad thing. YHWH promises to make the names of both Abraham and David great. However, in contrast to the name of Abraham and David made great by YHWH, who is doing the name making at Babel? They are. They're attempting to make their own name great for themselves by aligning with gods who will give them the power they crave.

Second, and related to the first, the motivation for stewarding power in the way of Babel was security. We see this in the justification "so that we won't be dispersed over all the earth" (11:4). In those days, people groups would disperse either due to expansion (cf., Gen. 1:28) or due to a scarcity of resources.[4] They sought to establish their power hold as a means of establishing their economic security in the land. All done without dependence upon YHWH.

The building of the tower necessarily involved an upward ascent, one to reach to the heavens in order to ascend to the places of the gods. It formed a hierarchal structure where only the priestly class were likely to ascend to the very top, where a bedroom would have been constructed for the descending deities to find respite. There the priests would furnish the bedroom with food and wine to refresh the deities.[5]

The problem with upward ascents is that for one to ascend upward through human effort, it must be with a boot on the neck of someone else. One ascends upward in Babel's power by stepping on the backs of others, ascending through the oppression of others. You and I can attain the power of Babel in very much the same way, especially over women, whose power is often the most vulnerable in both church and marketplace.

I have observed in many organizations how power brokers function in the way of Babel, not only cling to power itself, but also to how that power is distributed. Like the priestly class who would have undoubtedly limited access to the uppermost parts of the ziggurat to only a select few, so too Babel power brokers in organizations find their significance and safety through limiting who gets into what meetings, who has access to the church's green room, who is bought in on crucial decision making—and who hasn't. They know how to work around positional power structures—so that they are the type of person about whom people say, "well, [Boss] is in charge, but [Power broker] is *really* the one running the show."

---

4. Walton et al., *IVP Bible Background Commentary*, 42.

5. Walton et al., *IVP Bible Background Commentary*, 45.

Babel power brokers are often rife with an insecurity that drives them, as Villacorta notes, on an insatiable quest for affirmation and significance. Rather than finding it through Christ, they find it in accumulating power at the expense of those around them. Like President Alma Coin in *The Hunger Games*, Babel power brokers will often promise to accumulate their power with the intention to liberate and even bless the masses. But, also like Coin, once that power is achieved, and they find themselves enjoying the clean cool air whilst perched atop the ziggurat, they refuse to descend.

It's comfortable at the top of the ziggurat. The food is better. The wine is richer. The accoutrements are much more luxurious. All the people who built the ziggurat can look upon on and adore you as you commune with the divine in a way that only they could dream of. Who would want to descend from such a height only to mix among the common folk who built the structure?

Babel power always props up human-made hierarchies that benefit a few while oppressing many. The structure of the ziggurat itself, with a narrower peak than its wider base, is an architectural testimony to how Babel power works. And so often women find themselves toward the base of Babel power, suffering its oppressive consequences. Babel power structures are inherently designed to steward power for the safety and significance of those at the top of the ziggurat. Andy Crouch says, "Our use of power will always be disordered and destructive—will result in idolatry and injustice—unless we find a way to a restored relationship with the Giver of power."[6]

POWER AS AN UNLIMITED RESOURCE: PASSOVER POWER

Scripture shows us a more excellent way to steward power. It is what Villacorta refers to as a "downward ascent"[7] or the way of weakness or "powerlessness."[8] In that, Villacorta doesn't mean that God is absent of power but rather that the testimony of Scripture shows us a God who consistently and regularly demonstrated his power through confounding displays of weakness. We see this downward ascent of power described in Paul's words to the Philippians:

> Though he was in the form of God, he did not consider being
> equal with God something to exploit. But he emptied himself by

6. Andy Crouch, *Playing God*, 9, as quoted in Villacorta, *Tug of War*, 42.

7. Villacorta, *Tug of War*, 26–27.

8. Villacorta, *Tug of War*, 13.

> taking the form of a slave and by becoming like human beings. When he found himself in the form of a human, he humbled himself by becoming obedient to the point of death, even death on a cross. Therefore, God highly honored him and gave him a name above all names, so that at the name of Jesus everyone in heaven, on earth, and under the earth might bow and every tongue confess that Jesus Christ is Lord, to the glory of God the Father. (Phil 2:6–11)

It is a paradox indeed. Though Jesus was equal to God, that equality was not "something to exploit" (2:6) during his earthly ministry (i.e., Babel power). His demonstration of power through weakness was so consistent throughout his earthly ministry that the tale of his power stewardship reaches its climactic point atop the hill called Golgotha, where Jesus demonstrated the ultimate downward ascent of power.

But then Paul continues that it was *therefore*—because of Jesus' humble obedience in powerlessness—that God bestowed upon him the name above all names. It was through the triumph of his powerlessness on the cross that the victory of his resurrection was won. Now, the humble suffering servant sits enthroned over all creation, not ruling as a tyrant perched atop the ziggurat but with a power that flows downward to benefit even the most marginalized and overlooked. The power of Jesus is not to conquer the nations but to bring healing to them (cf., Rev 22:2).

We find this power/powerlessness paradox on display most profoundly in the events of the final Passover meal Jesus shared with his disciples before his betrayal and subsequent crucifixion. Of this event Villacorta says, "Jesus is simply showing the way of service is rooted in a place of powerlessness, not an upward path but a downward pull."[9]

What profound imagery to describe what I have affectionately called "Passover Power." Unlike the upward path that characterizes Babel power, Passover power pulls power downward. It is demonstrated most acutely in the image of the Creator and rightful King of all the universe bending with a towel and basin at hand to wash the feet of his followers—including one who would betray him before the night was out. Babel power perches a powerful few atop the masses, sucking all power into their own life force like one of the dementors from the *Harry Potter* series, rendering the masses helpless.

By contrast, Passover power pulls its power from the source of all power: God himself. Unlike the limited resource that is Babel power, Passover power is limitless, because God himself is omnipotent. While Babel power functions like a basin—hoarding human power for its own use, Passover

---

9. Villacorta, *Tug of War*, 24.

power turns the powerful into conduits, pulling the power of God down toward those who are often found on the margins: the disabled, the infirm, the poor, children, and *women*. Babel power treats power like pie—if I have more, you must have less. Passover power treats power as an infinite gift we can give away, even when it causes us to appear weak—for when we are weak, we are indeed shown strong (2 Cor. 12:10).

PASSOVER POWER AND WOMEN

Throughout my years in church ministry, I've found that men and power have a unique relationship. Typically speaking, we do not like to appear weak, though the visible powerlessness of Passover power is precisely what Scripture beckons us to do. Modern depictions of what it means to have biblical masculinity often invoke images of Babel power—men who must be stern, stoic, and overly confident in their own opinion. But Babel power has nothing to do with a biblical depiction of what it means to be a man, least of all when we look at the character of Jesus, who was given the name above every name yet did not consider equality with God as something to exploit.

Real manhood looks like Passover power. When we look in the gospels at Jesus' treatment of women, we see that Passover power was his *modus operandi*. The Samaritan woman at the well, the woman caught in the act of adultery, the woman who anoints Jesus' feet at Bethany, Mary sitting at his feet, and the list goes on and on. Encounter after encounter with the women, we find a Jesus who stewarded power in a downward ascent. He did not spend any time telling women their rightful place—in fact, he appears to upend those cultural assumptions. He did not devote his energy or leverage his standing in the community to policing women to keep them down. Instead, he lifted them up.

Jesus used his power to defend women.

Jesus used his power to advocate for women.

Jesus used his power to empower women.

And Jesus sent the Holy Spirit so that our daughters would have power to prophesy.

For men then, we should not see Passover power—a power of powerlessness, a strength found in weakness—as lacking in masculine strength, unless we are willing to say that Jesus lacked such masculine strength. I, for one, am not. Instead, Jesus gives us the ideal model of manly treatment toward woman. Manly men stewarding their power do not wield it to oppress women but use it to liberate them.

Was Jesus frequently criticized for his stewardship of power? Certainly. The religious leaders and even his own disciples often failed to understand why Jesus did the things he did, especially concerning women. But Jesus did it anyway.

Hear me: if you're a man and you choose Passover power in your treatment of women, you will be misunderstood. People will call you weak. They will crack jokes about your wife running the show or wearing the pants in the family. They'll call you a "beta male." They'll feel their camo and monster truck masculinity is superior to your gentle and lowly masculinity. But take heart: Passover power is the way of Jesus. And the reality is, you can still hunt and watch monster truck rallies and eat your steak raw and embrace Passover power. You can be the man God has created you to be while stewarding the power he has given you to liberate and lift up the women in your life. Ultimately, as we shall see, Babel loses.

THE FALL OF BABEL

Babel power is all around us. It's how people cultivate fortune and fame. It's how they amass empires of industry. It's how they are seemingly adored by throngs of fans and possess everything they could ever want. Babel power feels magnificent. Who doesn't want to sit atop the ziggurat and be thought of as communing with the divine, receiving special revelation over which the masses fawn? Who doesn't want to be the guy with all the answers who orders people to and fro?

But the Babel described to us doesn't exist anymore.

Why? Because the empires built with human hands always come crashing down. Only that which is built by the way of the Kingdom endures forever. And not only did Babel fail, but it failed swiftly and miserably.

We find in Gen 11 that the people did indeed build a city and the Babel ziggurat at its center. At the peak of that tower, the gods summoned by the powerful were expected to descend and commune, give the powerful instruction and blessing—which they in turn would distribute to the masses as they saw fit.

But Babel's gods didn't come down.

Just as quickly as they finished the city (somewhere, presumably, between verses four and five), YHWH himself came down.

YHWH came down, and he broke up the band. He undid their efforts to amass power from other gods and scattered the proud and the powerful throughout the earth (cf. Mary's *Magnificat* in Luke 1:51–53). Babel power is ultimately rooted in a desire for power and in control—to be as God himself is, just without God. Babel power assumes that to ascend to the heavens, to sit enthroned with the stars, to have one's boot on the necks of the masses is to be like the most high. But this was the assumption of Lucifer, and it ultimately led to his undoing (Isa 14:12–14).

Babel power ultimately fails because God himself is opposed to it. We should behave in kind, abhorring power amassing for the benefit of a few at the center and rather favoring the distribution of God's power to lift up the many on the margins, including women.

STEWARDING PASSOVER POWER

If Babel is doomed to fail, we must ask ourselves what stewarding Passover power looks like in the real world, specifically as it pertains to women. The answer is simple to articulate but difficult to walk out. Passover power inevitably requires dying to one's flesh, sacrificing for the sake of our sisters, and signing up for a life of being perpetually misunderstood.

First, we should understand the difference of how power flows between Babel power and Passover power. Babel power flows in a manner that is all-too-familiar to us:

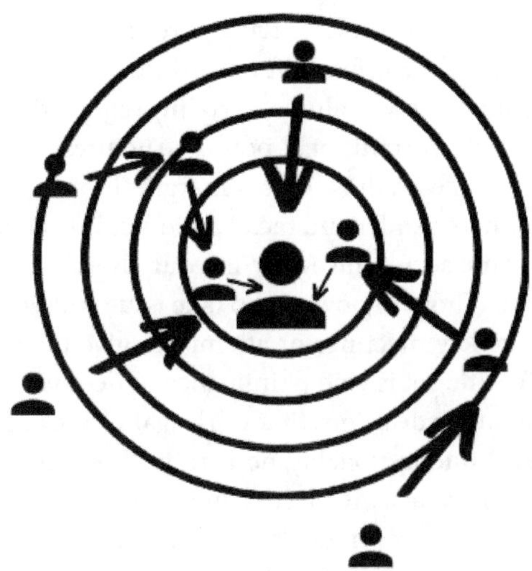

As the figure illustrates, in a Babel power system, power is redistributed from those on the margins toward those in the inner circle. The closer you are to the inner circle, the more power you have, terminating with the person(s) at the top of the organization. But now let's look at a basic Passover power structure:

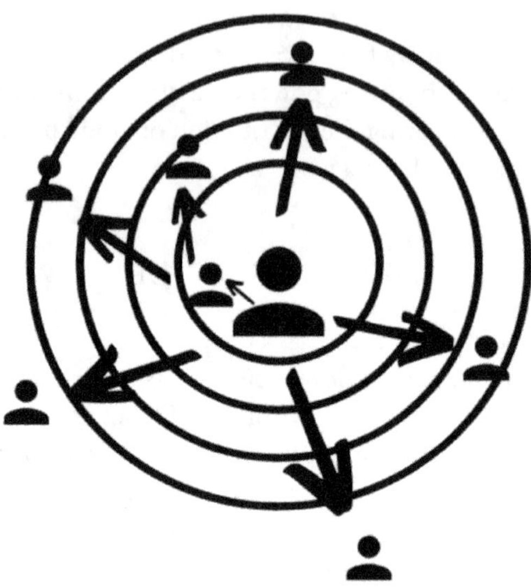

In a Passover power structure, leadership recognizes its presence is to serve those entrusted to them. Pay attention to the differences in the first two figures. First, one of the inner circle figures is missing in the Passover power structure. That's because a shift toward this form of power stewardship within an organization will almost certainly require that some in power need to transition out. In traditional power structures, there will be some that simply cannot deal with those on the margins having a newly amplified voice—especially where gender and racial prejudices are concerned. Do you want to uncover some secret misogyny in your church or business? Begin to empower women. Those in power who take issue with it will begin to cut those women out of key meetings or attempt to give them a position that possesses a fanciful title yet is void of influence or decision making capability. They will make subtle decisions that work against the moves to empower women. And they'll unquestionably need to be corrected or they'll likely need to leave. If you are a senior leader in an organization, and you can't seem to figure out when women don't feel empowered, your issue likely resides among those in the circles of authority closest around you.

Another change between the two figures: notice how in the Passover power figure more (though not all) of the arrows point directly from the senior leader to those on the margins? This is not to suggest that senior leaders should ignore organizational structures—that breeds chaos. But it does mean that senior leaders should establish practices and processes to hear from those on the margins of the organization. To elevate their *voice* if not their position.

One such example was in a church I served in several years ago in which I was tasked with helping to craft the church's new core organizational values. I was invited to a meeting that consisted of myself and two other people—all of us in senior leadership positions within the organization. My advice to the leader running the meeting was that we needed to pause. We needed to involve individuals from every level of the organization to give input into what our values were. If the values did not arise from the voice of the whole, they would need to be imposed upon the whole—and while you *can* impose values on others, you cannot impose their sincere and personal adoption of those values. They'll just fake it to make it. Getting a sense of the lived, incarnational values of an organization only comes through a collaborative process where everyone feels they've been given a voice, either directly or through representation.

Unfortunately, my advice was ignored in favor of a speedy resolution to the project and, as I predicted, those values may now appear on the employee handbook somewhere, but are not a part of the lived ethos of the organizational culture—simply because the process of giving voice to those on the outer rings of power was not done. Speedy solutions to problems rarely give voice to those who are not already in the room.

However, the ideal Passover power scenario would adopt the principle of the Parable of the Unforgiving Servant in Matt 18:21–35, where those who are empowered would recognize they have been entrusted with much and empower others in kind. Such a scenario would be multi-directional, with those even who have previously been deprived of power stewarding in the Passover manner of Jesus. In this way, the Spirit's power can move with even greater ease through communities of believers, as they recognize the unfathomable depths and boundless heights of the power that comes from the Source of all power.

PASSOVER POWER FROM AUTHORITY AND FROM WEAKNESS

When looking to affect change in the power dynamics of an organization, we must recognize that some of that change can be affected from a place of positional authority while some of it must be affected from a place of relative weakness. The incredible thing about Passover Power is there is little difference in *whether* change can be affected from a place of authority or weakness. Instead, the difference is in *how* that change is affected.

In their work on instituting change through the Christian communities, *Faith-Rooted Organizing*, Alexia Salvatierra and Peter Heltzel describe two types of mobilizing power, as described in how Jesus commissions his disciples to engage the world: wise as serpents and innocent as doves (Matt 10:18). To understand the meaning of "serpent" here, you must detach it from our culture's imagery of a serpent as a symbol of evil and cunning and return it to the biblical culture's association of a serpent with wisdom and even healing. When Salvatierra and Heltzel speak of "Serpent power," they refer to power that is wielded through "power of force, wealth, social influence, and numbers."[10] It is power from a place of human capacity or authority.

Dove power, by contrast, is a power that taps into what the Spirit of God is doing in the hearts and lives of people before we even get there. It is manifested in the power of appealing to moral authority, to the work of the Spirit within the souls of women and men, and in the power of prayer. Of this, the authors state,

> The Holy Spirit is ever at work on each of us, pulling and pushing for the victory of the best within us. Through nonviolent direct action and faith-centered moral dialogue, we can be an ally of the Spirit in its work on the soul of the person in power. We can awaken powerful people to their deeper calling and responsibility to share power.[11]

While Babel and Passover speak to power systems, Dove power and Serpent power speak to the means by which change is affected within those systems. Both Dove and Serpent power can be tools for affecting change within a Babel system to reform it toward a Passover system. This often involves mobilizing coalitions of change in both prayer (Dove power) and in leveraging the numeric and positional influence of the coalition to press for change (Serpent power). Change agents within organizations can appeal to the humanity of a Babel leader for change (Dove power) or change agents can organize to demand change from that leader (Serpent power).

As it pertains to reforming church and marketplace organizations alike, men are positioned uniquely to organize and mobilize for the greater empowerment of women, simply because they are more often the ones in positions of power. Patriarchal leaders often expect women to buck at oppressive policies or inequal treatment, and they have an abundance of

10. Salvatierra and Heltzel, *Faith-Rooted Organizing*, 74.

11. Salvatierra and Heltzel, *Faith-Rooted Organizing*, 78.

excuses prepared to justify them. I recall once when one such leader sat with Tara who was on staff at a church and asked what position she foresaw herself stepping into in the future within the church. When she told him that she foresaw herself growing into an executive leader role, the patriarchal leader was prepared with reasons why "everyone" wants to be in executive leadership but how the real work of the ministry was done "at the bottom." She left, feeling gaslit for being honest about her career goals and made to feel like her decade and a half of pastoral ministry and multiple seminary degrees were somehow to be viewed as equal to less mature men who were fresh out of college with similar ambitions. After telling her that there was "no more room" in the church for "people like her," this patriarchal leader at an egalitarian church made attempts to demote her into a role she could have done in a volunteer capacity.

But when men in power stepped into the situation, it upended the whole thing. Tara ended up being elevated because other men within the organization were willing to step in and advocate for her. It is not that there is any particular inherent *quality* with men in such situations that gives them greater advantage to bring justice, but there is an inherent *privilege* that affords a power to do so. Is it right? No, but privilege rarely is. The point of the matter is not that men should feel shame for our privilege in organizations, but instead we should recognize it for what it is: a form of power rooted in our gender, and we should use it to lift others up. Male privilege can be a stumbling block for women or it can be a stepping stool, and we get to choose how we want to use it. We can actually use the systemic prejudices woven into the DNA of the organizations in which we work *for the precise purpose* of undoing the systemic prejudices woven into the DNA of the organizations in which we work. The question remains whether we *want* to lay down our crowns and scepters at the feat of the One who showed us the right way to steward power: not as something to exploit but as something to drive from the halls of powerful men into the hands of women.

Chapter 5

The Smoking-Hot Wife

We've all heard it at one time or another—a well-meaning (male) pastor takes the microphone and introduces his "smoking-hot wife, [Insert Name]." It's a tale as old as time. Well, perhaps not as old as *time*. But it has become something that has occurred so frequently as to arise to a mythic proportion that warranted my naming the title of this chapter after it. While responses to these moments range from an obligatory giggle to quiet, internalized rage, the smoking-hot wife moment is a real moment in evangelical spaces. And even though it's become something of a joke now, it still happens. In fact, some pastors I've spoken to double down on this performative act as one of heart-felt praise for their wives. Why is this?

What I've come to call the "smoking-hot wife effect" is not relegated only to this variety of cringeworthy public praise. We men have a terrible habit of doing things to our wives, and to other women, often out of a sincere desire to *help*. But instead, we *hurt*. It may be a subtle form of hurt—so subtle that even our wives may not immediately recognize how something as simple as declaring how "smoking-hot" she is to a room full of people who didn't come there to objectify her actually undermines her as a woman as well as in whatever position she holds within the church. In general, humans have a profound capacity to inflict unintentional hurt in the name of helping.

Cherie found herself at the receiving end of a variation of the smoking-hot-wife effect when she was promoted to campus pastor at the megachurch at which she served for well over a decade. Equipped with the exceptional blend of enormous administrative and strategic capacity and a skilled shepherd's heart cultivated both by years of pastoral ministry and the education to undergird it, Cherie sat in a meeting where a senior leader announced her new role. But when the leader began to elaborate about why she was the right fit for the role, he described how the role was shifting to be more administratively-oriented and also, it satisfied the need to promote a woman into a higher position, so it was a win-win. In the mind of the leader, he was describing the reasons why Cherie was the ideal fit, but in doing so actually served to undermine her by insinuating that in other circumstances they would have looked for a different (male) person. His attempt at helping actually hurt. This is the smoking-hot wife effect.

In my world (missiology), hurting-while-helping is a criticism levied at short-term missions trips. A well-meaning, passionate group of Christians from the West travel to a remote part of the world and build a school or dig a well for the nationals in the name of helping. What they don't realize is that this effort to help often deprives nationals of jobs, tradespeople of the capacity to sell the goods needed to build whatever is being built, and much more. The desire to help doesn't always mean we are helping.

In this chapter, I want to look at several ways men can, in the name of trying to empower women, actually undermine or disempower them. I've leaned on the input of a number of women to hopefully address areas in which I even have blind spots as I write this. The point of this chapter is not to make men feel shame but to uncover areas in which our best-laid plans to elevate our wives and other women serve to do the opposite. Afterall, our best of intentions ultimately don't matter if what we're making things worse. It's also worth noting that by no means is this list exhaustive or that all women perceive these trespasses equally (or even as trespasses at all!). But if we can reach a point, at the end of this chapter, where we cultivate some awareness of how our actions impact women, we will have done good work.

PRAISING HER LOOKS TOO MUCH

This is the smoking-hot wife effect in its true form. Christian men have been conditioned to view ourselves as exceedingly "visual creatures" (so much so that we assume it is a biological fact when it is actually a culturally-conditioned one). Therefore, we often resort to compliments about the physical form of our wives when we desire to praise her. I believe this is most often done from the heart of a man who simply wants his wife to feel good about herself and to publicly acknowledge his adoration for her. Remarks like this, whether from the platform, in a group, or on a social media post, can range anywhere from a playful mention all the way to more detailed, sexualized set of remarks that could make a sailor blush. I've heard men remark from the platform about what they want to do to their wives when they get home and more. The brashness of the sentiment is intended to be edgy and fly in the face of a more Victorian-era regard concerning pulpit conduct. And while I'm sympathetic to the fact that Scripture is far more explicit in some ways than would ever be considered acceptable from the average American church pulpit (cf., Ezek 16; 23), there are a host of issues with an overabundance of physical and overly-sexualized comments about your wife (or, heaven forbid, other women) in public settings.

First, the *way* we praise the physical appearance of another speaks a great deal to how we view our spouse. It's one thing to refer to your wife as beautiful or lovely or some other adjective that describes her in a way that speaks of her as one whose presence enhances the beauty of God's good creation. It's quite another to objectify a woman—*even your wife*—especially when it is for public consumption. The foundational difference is that remarks about beauty ultimately concern part of a woman's created virtue. Remarks about her sex appeal relegate her to a commodity—a good to be consumed like anything else. It actually diminishes her worthiness rather than enhances it.

Rich Villodas speaks to this as he outlines the three different types of "diets" of sexual formation: starvation, fast-food, and banquet. Starvation is essentially what the church has promoted for much its history: the exaltation of the soul at the expense of the body. In the view of a starvation diet, proper sexuality is one which deprives the body of sex so the soul can flourish. This is why many church fathers relegated even *marital* sex as something to be done only for procreative purposes.

The fast-food diet is the opposite. It is the deprivation of the soul so the body can flourish. At its core, "smoking-hot wife" praise is a reaction against the starvation diet but wades dangerously close to fast-food sexual diet. If it's not McDonald's, it's most definitely Applebee's (i.e., fast-food adjacent).[1] It is a cheapening of what God intended for human sexuality to be in its fullness.

Instead, Villodas calls for a banquet approach to our sexual formation that views the body and soul as conjoined and inseparable, and human sexuality as a God-given beauty that transcends genital sex (more on that later). A banquet sexuality does not deny that we are inherently sexual creatures, nor that our wives are.[2] But that our sexuality and theirs are profoundly

1. Villodas, *Deeply Formed Life*, 113–17.
2. Villodas, *Deeply Formed Life*, 117–18.

deeper and more connected in union to God than flippant praise about her body or what you might do to it once church is over.

A second, related, reason why I caution against sexualized praise is what it says to other women in the room. What men don't often realize is that, because of the social conditioning of what constitutes beauty, when women hear another woman being praised for her looks, they naturally begin to assess all the ways in which they are *not* like the woman in question. So, when a man starts praising his wife's "hot bod," women in the congregation assess their own bodies against hers. It is tragic fruit born from a culture that praises unattainable aspirations of beauty, but it is a reality nevertheless. Is this how we should use the pulpit? Is this how we want to treat other women around us? To speak about our wives as beautiful in a "banquet sexuality" way (to use Villodas' terminology), doesn't invite these same self-objectifying and shaming practices like overly sexualized comments do.

Third, I've had several conversations in which male pastors speak about the practice of praising their wife's looks publicly as being an effort to reinforce their status as an "off-market" commodity. It is, in their view, a subtle way to remind the other women in the room that he is taken—so best you not try anything, ladies! I chuckle while even committing this description to paper because it is utterly and completely ridiculous. I'm not suggesting that there aren't *ever* women in a congregation that are on the prowl or who try to seduce pastors. But even a cursory glance at the headlines around pastoral sexual abuse demonstrate that it is overwhelmingly most often male pastors who are taking a predatory sexual posture in churches.

Fundamentally this reasoning is flawed because first—and I know this is difficult for many of us men to deal with—most women aren't after you. It's true. Our egos inflate our own sense of our desirability far beyond reality. Second, if the motivation is to use praise toward your wife as a sort of stick to keep all the women in your congregation at bay, may I submit for consideration that this is an impure motive for praising your wife? Third and last, the motivation to praise one's wife for such a reason betrays an underlying perspective of cross-gendered relationships that is overly sexualized and in need of redemption.

Finally, overly sexualized remarks about one's wife disempower the other fine attributes for which you've grown to love your wife. Why not, instead of praising her derrière, praise her mind? Praise her strength. Her independence. Her discernment. These things actually fit within the framework of what makes a woman beautiful, so praising her beauty pairs nicely with them.

I confess that long ago I was once a part of the "smoking-hot wife" brigade. But I found, as years went on (and through a great deal of longsuffering and feedback from Tara) that I could publicly praise Tara out of a genuine posture in a way that heaped praise upon her *and* actually subtly edified other women in the process.

I intentionally identified and praised those *virtues* I loved in Tara: strength, fortitude, perseverance, discernment, wisdom, intelligence, etc. These (and more) are virtues men and women alike can cultivate. A focus on edifying her, as well as others in our congregation, on the basis of their virtues rather than their appearance served to upend and, hopefully, rewrite culturally-conditioned scripts for what womanhood should be. Beauty is not a set of measurements, skin tone, or style of dress. Beauty is the cultivation of virtues that transcend outward appearance and endure throughout the course of a woman's whole life. That is what is worthy of praise.

Men, it is worth adding that it is helpful to identify and seek to emphasize virtues and characteristics that aren't just those that are typically thought to be "feminine" (e.g., grace, poise, motherhood, how she helps you, etc.). Break the stereotypes and get creative. Praise her wit, her ability as a teacher or preacher, her theological mind, her passion for the gospel, and more.

NARCISSISTIC PRAISE

Another manner in which men hurt while thinking they're helping is in the manner by which we praise women. Unlike the oversexualization of compliments, which are (hopefully) only an issue with one's spouse, narcissistic praise is not limited only to how we praise our spouse. It can be a co-worker, someone who works under us, or another close friend or family member. It's also not a practice that only men do to women. But for our purposes, we'll limit the scope to just that.

We've all seen narcissistic praise given in one way or another. It's likely we've all given some narcissistic praise, too. It is a compliment, an observation, or a tribute given to honor someone that actually ends up being more about the *giver* of the compliment than the object of it. It is how the person impacts *them*, what they mean to *them*, what the presence of that person means in *their* life—perhaps even with a personal story or two thrown in. You can observe narcissistic praise often in the obligatory tributes given on social media—a post a husband makes about his wife's birthday, their anniversary, or some other event. It can be at an event such as a birthday party or a celebration for a life accomplishment. No matter how hard the guy tries, somehow the praise seems to be more about him than it does her!

This happens in organizational settings as well. A male boss may give a public shoutout to one of his employees by detailing at length what a benefit she has been to him or how much easier she has made his life. A pastor may speak at length about how his wife makes him look or feel to the congregation. Or in an illustration, he may consistently use her as the character who required growth as he remains the wise sage.

Narcissistic praise is a close sibling to narcissistic conversation. A normal, healthy conversation typically goes like this:

> Person 1: "X happened to me."
>
> Person 2: "[Insert empathizing statement]. [Ask probing question in response]?"
>
> Person 1: "[Answers probing question in response to Person 2]. [Ask question about Person 2's perspective]."

But narcissistic conversation may go something like this:

> Person 1: "X happened to me."
>
> Person 2: "Oh tell me about it, once Y happened to me."
>
> Person 1: "Oh my gosh, no kidding. Once Z also happened to me."

Do you see the difference? In the healthy conversation there is genuine dialogue—two people speaking with one another. In narcissistic conversation, however, the conversation essentially amounts to two monologues happening in proximity to one another. The other person ceases to be someone to understand, but is merely a listening board against which I may bounce the soundwaves of my own experience. The same is true in narcissistic praise. The other person ceases to be an object of adoration and congratulation, but a filter through which I can reflect on my own self-absorbed experience.

Is personal reflection when giving praise always inappropriate? Of course not. But there is such a thing as too much of it. And if men are not careful, they can make the praise they intend to laud upon a spouse, co-worker, or female friend into something that tells your hearers more about *you* than it does about *her.* Just as too much salt can eventually ruin your favorite dish, so also too much self-reflection can ruin your compliment.

CAPPING HER POTENTIAL

When Tara and I were first in ministry, I loved the fact that she was walking out her calling to be a pastor. It is what we both envisioned our lives would be like—arm-in-arm, making a difference for the kingdom together. For several years that followed, however, I found myself having small flare-ups of jealousy after she would preach an incredible sermon. I got annoyed when her preference for handling a church situation a certain way turned out to be the right one. Unbeknownst to me at the time, my ego cultivated an inferiority complex within me that began to bear bad fruit in our marriage and ministry. If I were to have been honest with myself at the time, I was fine with Tara flourishing in her potential, so long as her potential didn't exceed mine. When she appeared to outshine me, my fragile male ego simply couldn't handle it.

Our ego is certainly one way we cap the potential of women in our lives. But it is not the only way. In speaking with women around the country, I received scores of stories of odd ways women have felt capped by male superiors. Because of Tara's and my vocation as pastors, many of those stories come from female pastors. One pastor, named Jill, told me:

> I've never been given the opportunity to speak on a large platform, despite ample opportunities to do so elsewhere (Sunday school classes, women's groups, youth), and despite my requests for feedback on my speaking and teaching, I've received no critiques. My lead pastor is eager to see me speak and teach in these smaller forums but has not given me much to go off of to learn or grow from them, unfortunately, even though I've asked.

In this particular situation, it was the limited perspective of the lead pastor that capped Jill's potential. She was "good enough" for smaller venues but never for the big stage on a Sunday. Yet without the necessary feedback and training to improve those skills, how is Jill expected to improve in her preaching? In fact, the limited capacity to receive mentorship and training—either due to the lack of more senior female leadership within the church or the church's denomination, or because male superiors did not feel comfortable meeting one-on-one to coach or train the women—was noted by many of the women I spoke to.

In one egalitarian denomination, multiple women noted how the denomination frequently conflated pastoral training for female pastors with ministry to male pastor's *wives*. Sarah provides one such example:

> During [denominational events], [leadership holds] a lunch
> for pastors wives but then shoe horn[s] women with minister's

credentials. The devotional there has nothing to do with women ministers and they just talk about how hard being a pastors wife is. (Which yes, it is absolutely but it doesn't affect women who are in ministry without their husbands or, like me, are unmarried).[3]

Is being a wife of a pastor difficult? Absolutely. It's a weird concoction of roles with very little recognition for the work done—usually, for free. But it is also quite different from being a woman who is a pastor. They're simply different callings with markedly different needs for a denomination or other governing body to address. In a conversation years ago with a prominent female pastor, she recalled one specific gathering of the leadership of a church network to which her church belonged, where the women were all sent to a room where the network had hired a personal chef to give the women cooking classes. The men went into another room and to talk business. This pastor recalled profound frustration that she was sent away from the room she *needed* to be in so that she could be in the room network leadership thought she *should* be in. Tara and I experienced a similar encounter when training to be church planters, when a group of us in training together were separated by gender. The women were brought into another room and taught how to keep their man happy (which, of course, included matters of sexual fulfillment, keeping the house in order, etc.) so he can do the work of the ministry.

But Sarah notes another reason for which women are capped in ministry—marital status. For a woman to be single in church ministry is a more significant issue than a woman in the marketplace. Phoebe and Sandi both illustrate this with their experiences:

> [Phoebe:] I was hired on as a staff pastor when I was single. I met my husband and we got married and began to do some ministry together within the church. My husband got the call to preach and began to preach and fill in at our church. Meanwhile, at the time, I had been preaching, teaching and on staff for four years there. Long before my husband came along. Realizing my husband now has a call to preach, my pastor then says to me "I guess I will have to change your training to teaching you to be a pastor's wife instead of a pastor yourself." Without ever asking me if I wanted to step down from ministry, which I do not! The goal is that my husband and I will co-pastor together, not for me to step aside because he is the man and now he has the call.[4]

3. Personal correspondence, Jun 27, 2022.
4. Personal correspondence, Jun 27, 2022.

[Sandi:] [In] my first full-time ministry position, I was the college and young adult pastor. I was [young] and single. Things were going well although I was (very casually) informed that I was hired because I was a single woman so they wouldn't have to pay much. I was engaged shortly after so I requested a raise for no other reason than that I would soon be married. I was told that it was an unrealistic reason for a raise. That in "the real world" people don't get paid more for being married. I responded that people also are not usually paid less just because they are single. Surprisingly, I got the raise.[5]

Examples like these are unthinkable in the marketplace—at least that a leader would have the boldness to outright admit to discrimination based on gender or marital status to an employee. But it is a commonplace experience for single women in church vocations, as many church staffs do not meet the employee quantity thresholds for such discrimination to be enforceable by the Equal Employment Opportunities Commission (EEOC).

While our egos get in the way of a woman reaching her full potential, our lived policies do as well. How we treat women solely based on their gender or marital status has very real and very significant implications for how their potential to walk out their calling is capped. We may think we're helping by doing things like putting female pastors and pastor's wives together for a brunch "so the ladies all have something to talk about." But in those instances, our desire to help actually hurts.

THE MOTHER'S DAY AND WOMEN'S CONFERENCE CIRCUIT

The Mother's Day and Women's Conference preaching circuit is an issue exclusively in the church world but one that deserves attention nevertheless. Every year, scores of male pastors in egalitarian churches, when planning through the preaching calendar for the year, come to Mother's Day and think to themselves, "Ooh! We gotta get a woman to preach that day." Then, in planning to host their annual women's conference, many pastors think to themselves or say to their staff, "Ooh! We gotta get a woman to preach that day." Then, as quickly as the thought of having a woman preach came, it drifts away only to return again next year when it's time to fill the pulpit on Mother's Day and during the annual women's conference.

There are two issues with this. First, for those of us in churches who believe in the full participation of women in their calling to be pastors, it's

5. Personal correspondence, Jun 27, 2022.

simply lazy to only have women preach on Mother's Day or only speak during women's conferences. It is not only insulting to women—who are more than capable of preaching outside of the month of May; it lacks imagination. Pastor, hear me: your church needs the feminine voice within it to not only preach and teach, but to help shape the vision of your church. As we noted in an earlier chapter, God's created design for men and women was that they would steward sacred space together. While that doesn't necessitate men and women to necessarily co-pastor (though I personally believe this is an ideal leadership scenario for a church), it does mean that the male and female voices of your church should be heard equally. As such, women should—at a bare minimum—preach quarterly, if not monthly, from the pulpit of an egalitarian church.

The second issue, which is actually resolved by resolving the first issue, is that I don't think women should preach on Mother's Day.

There. I said it. It's the one day of the year that I actually think it's wiser to have a man in the pulpit. But why?

Because I'm completely convinced that the trend to have women preach on Mother's Day was an idea started by a group of male pastors. Because it could only be men who would act on the assumption that women would want to work—*on Mother's Day*. I'm confident that the same inspiration that causes men everywhere to buy their wives treadmills and toasters for Mother's Day is the same inspiration that gave us the obligatory woman in the pulpit on a day meant to give her some time to relax. After all, what says, "hey, why don't you kick your feet up and take some time for yourself" to a woman more than asking her to spend the hours in the preparation, anxiety, self-loathing, feelings of inadequacy, and mental and spiritual exhaustion that comprises the love-hate relationship most of us have with sermon preparation and delivery? This anxiety is especially pronounced when the preacher is only allowed to flex her preaching muscle once a year.

Now, I'm joking a little in my dogmatic insinuation—but only a little. I understand there is value in a church hearing from one of its mothers on Mother's Day. But I will say, when Tara and I co-pastored our church, we flipped the script. She preached Father's Day and I preached Mother's Day. It was sublime. But she was also in the pulpit (along with other women) more than many churches permit. But to my point, when women are frequently in a church's pulpit, it isn't as strange to find them absent one day a year—when they should be kicking up their feet.

Some men may read that and feel inspired, so let me prod a little more. Give *all* women in your church Mother's Day off. No women serving anywhere. Let the men do the heavy lifting. If your church policies prohibit men in the nursery (as some do), hire a babysitting service for that day or enlist the help of young girls in your youth or college ministry. If women are active within the church—directing its ministries, preaching from its pulpit, and giving shape to its vision—it's not so weird or awkward to tell them one day a year, "ladies, sit down . . . we've got this today." From the women I've spoken to, it sounds like a dream come true.

WOMEN IN ADMINISTRATIVE ROLES

As I noted in a previous chapter, some women flourish in administrative roles. But we're hurting women if we assume they *all* do. We also hurt women by assuming that being *good* at administration is the same as *flourishing*. Good leadership requires the need to distinguish when someone is *called* to do something from when they're just really *good* at something. I am good at bread baking, but I don't feel a calling to be a baker. I have a wealth of knowledge of Civil War history, but you won't see me in one of those live action reenactments of the Battle of Gettysburg. Talent is not the same as calling and many women are talented at administration, leading many leaders above them to assume they are called to be administrators. This is simply not the case. When women *only* fill administrative roles, then men are the ones left to craft the vision of the organization. And if only men craft the vision, patriarchy is sure to follow.

THE "DIRECTOR FOREVER" ROLE

The director forever role is another church specific issue. But you can tell a lot about what a church believes about female empowerment by looking at its website—not the "beliefs" page but the "staff" page. In egalitarian churches, women will often be given the titles of director or coordinator, despite possessing the qualifications of pastor. When all the women who work at a local church bear the title of director or coordinator but never pastor, this speaks to a top-heavy patriarchy that most likely stifles the empowerment of women. To give women the functional responsibilities of the pastorate but stripped of the title is a feature in both complementarian and egalitarian churches alike. Jill, who has held credentials for six years in her egalitarian denomination, described her experience on staff at her local church:

> [I] was hired on under the title of "Office Administrator" at a local church. My lead pastor at my church was once nearby when someone asked me the question, "Are you a pastor?" at a local

pastor's event and when I looked to him, not knowing how to respond, he responded "Yes!"

However, I've never been given that title anywhere else, including in front of our congregation. It is known that I am a "reverend" but I am otherwise just "Jill." Our lead pastor, associate pastor, and a couple other men that are not on staff, but serve either occasionally or regularly are referred to as "pastor so-in-so." None of the women who hold credentials and serve are called "pastor" whether they're on staff or not. I'm not included in pastor appreciation month, either, though it has been acknowledged that maybe in some fashion I ought to be . . . the compromise was to celebrate me on Administrative Professionals Day. Except, that occurred when COVID hit and everyone forgot about it.

It seems petty in American culture to argue over titles. I rarely refer to myself as "Dr. Todd Korpi" and never correct someone when they withhold that title from me, though in some cultures this is important. Therefore, many women do not openly speak about the issue or demand particular titles in their churches. Yet, privately they will vocalize how the deprivation of the title of pastor stings.

Like many in my particular branch of the Christian family tree (Pentecostalism), I don't care much about titles. I often refer to pastoral colleagues interchangeably by their title or by their first name, simply because in our society we value the diminished power distance that doing away with titles brings. Yet, I have also observed a very intentional practice that, while I may speak about male pastors without their title, I almost *never* do so with women. The female pastors in my church are *always* "Pastor so-and-so." Is that silly? Hardly. Because even in egalitarian churches, female ministers are still frequently regarded as second-class to their male counterparts. So, the insistence upon the bestowal of her title is a small, intentional step toward challenging that inequality. If calling female pastors by their title moves the culture of a church even an inch in the right direct, it is the right decision.

Some may argue that the women on their staff do not possess either the calling nor the qualifications in your denomination to bear the title. If it is a matter of calling—*she* has expressed that she does not feel called to be a pastor (not that you've simply assumed that is the case), that is one thing. But if it is a matter of qualification, the duty of a good senior pastor is to come alongside the women on his or her staff to help them take the necessary steps toward that qualification.

Women with whom I spoke noted another characteristic of unintentional disempowerment in their egalitarian churches related to titles. It is the opposite of the "director forever" role. Several noted that women are often given the title or office of a pastor and placed on boards, committees, staffs, etc. but are stripped of the decision-making power that grants them the capability to carry out the duties of the job. All *responsibility*, no *authority*. She may sit in the right meetings or possess the right job description, but organizational changes or political jockeying from her male counterparts make her role much harder to carry out.

I admit, during the first few years of our church planting and co-pastoring journey, this is what I unintentionally did to Tara. She bore the title of "lead pastor," and for the most part our congregation did a wonderful job of supporting her in that role. But I on the other hand struggled with insecurities that often deprived her of the authority to carry out her role without me. It wasn't until about a year and a half into our time there that I repented to her for holding so tightly onto authority that wasn't mine to hold, for the sake of my insecurity. And it took another year of me walking out that repentance before she genuinely felt like she had equality in our co-pastoring roles.

THE PUPPET QUEEN ROLE

In an episode of my favorite television shows, *The West Wing*, Roger Rees, playing the eccentric (possibly alcoholic) genius ambassador from the United Kingdom, Lord John Marbury, describes a British practice to keep the peace during the Empire's occupation of India:

> When we had a particular problem with someone, one solution we would try is to make him a maharajah. That's a kind of a regional king. We would pay him off with an annual tribute and in return he would be loyal to the crown.[6]

While I don't know how historically accurate Marbury's description is of British title making in India, the practice of rulers installing client kings to rule distant lands in their stead is well documented throughout human history. While I'm not a historian, I do know that as far back as the Hittite Empire, treaties were established between greater powers (called suzerains) and less powers (called vassals) in which the vassal was to be steadfastly loyal to the suzerain. This sort of suzerain-vassal agreement is much of the geopolitical drama that serves as the backdrop for the Old Testament book of Ezekiel. Nebuchadnezzar had deposed the ruling monarch of Judah, named Jehoiachin, and replaced him with a puppet named Zedekiah to rule as a loyal extension of Babylon. Often the most desirable trait of these

---

6. *West Wing*, "He Shall, From Time to Time."

ancient puppet rulers was not an ability to rule wisely or justly—but loyalty. Loyalty was valued above all.

As it pertains to women, the puppet queen role is when an unqualified woman is exalted into a position of influence or authority, for the sole reason that she is a woman. Her gender serves as her qualification, which serves the ultimate purpose of the organization appearing diverse. Lindsey spoke to me on this subject from her years in corporate America:

> I saw a lot of women promoted into leadership and management positions by an all-male executive staff who (after lawsuits and HR complaints) didn't want to be seen as discriminating against women. These women wanted positions they weren't ready for and hadn't been coached/trained properly for the positions they now held. Elevating a woman just because she is a woman backfires the same way elevating a man just because he is a man backfires. Many, many times these women ended up quitting entirely, stepping back into former positions, or being written up to the point of termination or demotion. Not only did the women suffer, but their staffs and the company as a whole suffered because of the turnover.[7]

As Lindsey notes, while elevation of any woman for any reason may appear like a good thing on the surface, when the woman is objectively unqualified and no training is provided to enhance her qualification, it does long-term damage to the egalitarian cause in that organization. It also does long-term damage to the woman herself, who is proverbially wearing Saul's armor.

While sometimes the exaltation of a puppet queen is done out of sincere motives, it is also often done to appease demands for genuine expressions of diversity. Whether those demands are external appearances or internal grievances, when puppet queens are installed in organizations, they are deprived of true empowerment and, like the client kings of yore, are expected to not create waves and just stay loyal to the leader.

A variation of the puppet queen role is a disempowered function, often within churches (though not exclusively) where women are paraded around in various public or stage roles, for the purpose of making church leadership appear as empowering. In this variation, the qualification of the woman is of no matter, because her feminine presence is all that is required. She is a puppet, but of a different variety—she has no formal authority like the normal puppet queen, but she is a token to give the illusion of diversity nonetheless.

7. Personal correspondence, Jun 27, 2022.

A WAY FORWARD

Some men may read this long treatment of ways we try to help but end up doing harm and feel discouraged or embarrassed at things we've done in the past. If you're like me, you may see some of your past self in them (or present self!). I would encourage you not to lose heart, however. It can be a daunting task to move beyond these mistakes into genuine empowerment, but it is possible. You will continue to mess up. I *still* have occasional conversations with Tara, where she voices a way in which my motive for helping to empower her was actually hurting. Living as humans with one another is like that. But it is worth the effort.

One first step is to identify ways you're currently disempowering the women closest to you, personally or professionally, by *asking* them. Don't get defensive when they honestly respond. Depending on how long the disempowerment has been going on and the nature of your relationship, they may not be completely forthcoming at first. That's ok. You will need to build trust through consistency over time with what little they give you. They may overload you with a host of things you could do better. Take note and begin to work on one or two. Don't focus on perfection, focus on consistency and humility.

The next step is to create additional, intentional feedback loops in your life that are feminine. Listening to women is important. But creating rhythms in your life through which you consistently seek out feedback from women is invaluable. And make tangible adjustments based on that feedback.

If you are the leader of a church, denomination, or some other type of organization, look at the leaders that surround you. Look at the leaders in the upper levels of your organization. Are there women in their ranks? If so, do those women feel empowered to speak truth to you or other sources of power in your organization? It's more important that *they* feel they are able to identify areas where women are disempowered than whether *you* feel they are able to do that. If the answer to these questions are no, today is a good day to begin to change that.

Chapter 6

Is Charles in Charge?

Most families wish to live in a harmonious, peaceful home environment that is full of love and respect for each other and a healthy sense of balance. Most people want good marriages, good relationships with their children, and to feel that their home is a place of peace and flourishing.

When Tara and I first got married, both of us twenty-two years old, we agreed that men and women were equal, both in the church and outside of it. One of the reasons I was so deeply attracted to Tara (and still am, for that matter!) was that her calling from God was uniquely *hers*. She wasn't simply a tagalong to whatever it was that I was up to. There was a healthy differentiation of self between us.

But like many young newlywed couples, we didn't realize just how large the secret cargo of baggage was that we were carrying with us into our new relationship. We each came of age in households that considered themselves egalitarian—in the church, in society, and in the home. But how we witnessed that egalitarian-ness lived out was quite another matter. For me, I observed my father for years serve coffee and tend to the logistics of the Sunday school classes my mother taught for years. He possessed a sort of humble reverence about it, too. In many ways, that image of my father still is buried in my egalitarian brain—a large, stoic Finnish man who hunted and fished and wrenched on cars, and who possessed a stereotypical masculinity that no one would scarcely challenge, given his intimidating size—yet he served my mom as she ministered in the church. But in our home, what I was brought up to believe was egalitarian wasn't always so. My parents certainly modeled an equality in decision making. Yet as it pertained to household duties, they reverted to traditional gender roles. My father performed all of the outside duties—mowing, fixing cars, etc., while my mother tended to all of the inside duties—cooking, cleaning, ironing, etc. I vividly remember frequent conversations my parents had before coming to church where my father asked my mother to iron a shirt for him, and she would subsequently oblige.

Tara's family was largely the opposite. Her parents shared inside and outside duties equally. Her father cleaned just as much as her mom tended to outside maintenance. Yet, as it pertained to decision making, her father retained sole power as the "head of the home." Her father insisted upon his right to grant permission for her mother, or Tara herself, to get their hair cut or colored and strictly enforced a similar sort of dress code as you would find in a fundamentalist Baptist or Pentecostal church.

I bring up these examples not in any way to disparage either of our upbringings. I only wish to underscore that despite the fact that we both entered marriage thinking we were egalitarian through and through, what we meant when we said the word "egalitarian" wasn't always what the other had in mind. I vividly remember the cool breeze that blew through our first home, a few weeks after our wedding, when I asked Tara why my shirts had not been ironed. She was appalled that I would ask such a question. I also didn't understand why she insisted upon me being involved in meal planning and preparation—despite both of us working full-time, I simply expected that she would take care of that. I didn't have a developed theology that insisted why she must bear that burden or why I must be the one to drive when we're in the car together. Rather, I imported what was particular to my upbringing into our new life together, assuming it was the how everyone lived.

We also occasionally reflect upon the absurdity of the first time she called me after we had been married a month or so to seek my permission to get her hair cut. When I told her it didn't matter to me whether she cut her own hair, her family background caused her to persist (lest she, so she thought, incur my wrath) by asking if I had any particular style or color preferences that I wanted or did not want. I had never heard my mother ask my father these sorts of questions.

These are just a few examples of the type of sorting out she and I had to do in order to establish our own "household codes" as a couple. When I refer to household codes, I refer to the underlying assumptions, ethics, and way of being that make up how a family functions. I'm happy to report that we both share in the load of cooking and cleaning and yard maintenance. Tara cuts and colors her hair however she chooses while, and I now much prefer to be the one who irons both of our clothes. It's not perfect—but that's part of the messy beauty of it all.

What I've come to observe over the years is that many people consider themselves egalitarian in the church. They believe women can serve in most or all areas of vocational ministry. Most people are egalitarian as it pertains to work. They believe women can and should work in any sector of society that they choose (though, as Beth Allison Barr observes, perhaps a majority don't believe in their heart that a women should be president[1]). Many of these same people may be egalitarian in the church, but there may be restrictions to that equality as it pertains to the home. My dissertation supervisor at Fuller Seminary, Betsy Glanville, refers to this as being "egalitarian but."

"Egalitarian but" has many forms. "I believe in women in ministry *but* women should only serve as staff pastors" (Never mind that there is absolutely no solid biblical support for this). "I believe women are equal, *but* they shouldn't do ____." "I believe women can serve in any area they desire, *but* it would be better if a man filled that role." And so on. "Egalitarian but" takes many forms, but the one I wish to focus on is Egalitarian at church (or work) *but* patriarchal at home.

EGALITARIAN AT CHURCH BUT PATRIARCHAL AT HOME

I suspect that most egalitarians are functionally patriarchal in the home. While they believe women and men can and should serve alongside one another, when they get home, the man is the head of the home. In speaking with many Christians over the years, I've found that for most, this is not a matter of a well-developed theology that insists upon a man's role being one to dominate and rule and a woman's role is to submit and be ruled over. Instead, it is often a default assumption because of cultural, societal, or religious assumptions and because complementarian household theology has dominated the Christian media landscape for years. The man has to be the head of the home because, well, Paul said so. Or because who else would do it? If a man is not the functional head of the home, as in the case of my parents who presided over our house as decision-making equals, then he is at least the *spiritual* head of the home. That is unquestionable truth.

Or is it?

It's worth looking at what Paul meant when he said that man is the "head." It's also worth looking at what we mean when we differentiate "spiritual" and "physical" when talking about headship. Finally, it's also worth

1. Barr, *Making of Biblical Womanhood*, 29–30.

looking at some practical considerations for what it means to function as an egalitarian household.

PAUL AND HEADSHIP

Many people have addressed Paul's use of the term head in both Eph 5 and 1 Cor 11, not least of which is N. T. Wright, who in an address to the Council for Biblical Equality in 2017 notes that the Greek term for head, *kephalē*, is one that is used in both a metaphorical sense and a literal sense. Wright insists that the term head in Paul's application with regard to men over women refers not to *authority* but to *source*.[2] So his line of thought does not refer to man as a head over woman, as in the head of an organization, but rather as the source of woman, as in the head of a river. In Wright's view, he is calling to mind the creation narrative. Wright suggests that Paul's treatment here is to encourage men and women to be uniquely themselves, as God designed, and not to blur the lines between them, as some gnostic sects may have been doing at the time, overextending Paul's meaning in Gal 3 where he says there "is no male and female" in Christ.

Another view holds that Paul is doing something similar in Eph 5 and 1 Cor 11 that he does in 1 Cor 6:12, where Paul says, "'I have the right to do anything,' you say—but not everything is beneficial. 'I have the right to do anything'—but I will not be mastered by anything." Jesus uses a similar technique in the gospels in his famous "You have heard it said, but I say unto you" phrasings, such as in Matt 5.

If this is the case, most modern translations have missed this and instead read patriarchy into the text. Ancient Greek and Hebrew did not have punctuation as we do today, so interpretation largely depended upon the readers' understanding of what the author was implying. But if Paul means a sort of "You have heard it said, but I say unto you" technique as he employs in 1 Cor 6, and as Jesus uses in in Matt 5, he is responding to and upending assumptions among his churches regarding the Roman household codes of the day—household codes the Corinthians and Ephesians would have understood as normal. Ephesians, for example, may be better understood as proceeding like this:

> Submit to one another out of reverence for Christ. [You have heard it said:] "wives, submit yourselves to your own husbands as you do to the Lord. For the husband is the head of the wife as Christ is the head of the church, his body of which he is

2. Wright, "Biblical Basis for Women's Service."

> the Savior. Now as the church submits to Christ, so also wives
> should submit to their husbands."
>
> [But I say unto you:] Husbands, love your wives, just as Christ
> loved the church and gave himself up for her . . . In this same
> way husbands out to love their wives as their own bodies . . .
>
> . . . However, each one of you must also love his wife as he loves
> himself and [in addition,] the wife must [continue to] respect
> her husband. (Eph 5:21–33, emphases mine)

I'm not suggesting that these words I'm inserting into the text be codified as Scripture, but their presence instead functions to give healthy context to what is likely actually Paul's argument (the same way we might infer, upon receiving a text message from a friend we're meeting that says "here," that he or she means "I'm here"). There would have been little reason for Paul to write to instruct wives to submit to their husbands. That was the *norm*. Men ruled women in ancient Rome. Where there was occasion, and would have likely been viewed as a threat to Roman family values, was that Paul was insisting that the *men* change how they viewed their wives. Wives were no longer to live as a procreation factory or a household manager, but an focus of adoration, affection, and sacrifice.[3]

While I favor this interpretation, I don't believe Paul would disagree with the theology undergirding Wright's interpretation of "head" either. It is deeply ironic that these two clobber passages, which have for years been prooftexts to keep women in their place, were likely two rather progressive challenges to the household codes of the day! Paul has elsewhere (e.g. Rom 16) established the regular pattern of women in church ministry. But here he tackles how the home is ruled. And, for Paul, the rulership of the home is decidedly egalitarian.

MAN AS THE SPIRITUAL HEAD

Many egalitarian people, both men and women, insist that while men and women can serve equally in ministry, and while men and women should functionally serve as equals in the home, that the man is still the spiritual head—the spiritual leader of his home. I'm sure some of you who read this are shocked that I might even challenge this idea: "Does he not want a man to be the spiritual head of his home?"

---

3. Peppiatt, *Rediscovering Scripture's Vision for Women*, 92–106; Barr, *Making of Biblical Womanhood*, 29–41.

But that's a silly notion, for a couple reasons. When I challenge the idea of male spiritual headship, people assume I mean to insist that men should abdicate that leadership position and women should assume it. But that's not what Scripture intends, either in the creation ideal of Gen 2, nor in Christ's reversal of the curse in Gen 3.[4] God's design is that men and women should steward sacred space as co-priests—in the church and in the home. So I don't mean to insist that men *aren't* the spiritual leaders of their homes. I only suggest that men and women are designed to do it *together*. It is together that the spiritual leadership of the home is set.

But the second problem is with the term "spiritual." The way "spiritual" is used in this context is in contrast to the physical. Men and women might do their finances, household chores, meal planning, etc., together—the *physical* things—but the *spiritual* matters are the domain of men—or at least where he might have the final say.

But this way of dividing the cosmos, between the unseen/spiritual/supernatural and the seen/physical/natural is born from the Enlightenment, not from Scripture. It is a way of dividing how we perceive reality that would have been entirely foreign to the cultures of the Bible and throughout most of human history. They rightly viewed *everything*, including that which is seen, physical, and natural, as inherently spiritual. God bringing about the birth of a child or the blooming of a flower were equally as spiritual as the parting of the Red Sea or Jesus' raising of Lazarus from the dead. Opening your home in hospitality to your neighbor is just as spiritual as proclaiming the gospel from a pulpit.

Instead, the ancients divided the world not by spiritual and physical, but by creator and creation. All of creation, both seen and unseen, corporeal and incorporeal, stood in contrast to its loving creator, who was intimately involved in its innerworkings—in both ways we can see and in ways we cannot see.

An entire book could be written on this subject alone, but it matters on the subject of the spiritual leadership of a home because we cannot rightly divide the "spiritual" from the practical as it pertains to leading the home. And God has called men and women to steward over all spiritual matters, both seen (e.g. commitment to a church, creation stewardship, etc.) and unseen (e.g. spiritual warfare, discernment, etc.) together as co-equals to the glory of God. Everything husbands and wives do together as they seek to build a home that honors God is a spiritual act. So to say that men and women should functionally lead the home together is to also say that men and women are equally the spiritual heads of their home.

4. Peppiatt, *Rediscovering Scripture's Vision for Women*, 50–55.

EGALITARIAN HOUSEHOLD CODES

Contrary to the Roman household codes of the day which saw the man as the ruler of his home, Paul appears to have suggested the upending of that hierarchy in the nascent Christian community. For Paul, it was not a flipping of the script, exchanging patriarchy for matriarchy. Instead, he sees the dismantling of human power dynamics in favor of living in the messy tension of Christian covenant together as co-equal husbands and wives. But Paul appears to take it even a step further—a step that, if I'm honest, I still wrestle with. Continuing into what we call chapter six, Paul continues to the same sort of "you have heard it said" dynamic and turns to the relationship even between children and parents—suggesting a level of egalitarianism in the relational dynamic between parents and children. This too would have struck his readers as incredibly odd. So how exactly does an egalitarian house function? At present I want to offer several suggestions.

Egalitarian Parenting

Egalitarian families seek to raise their children in a household where they grow to know they have full respect and dignity as equal human beings and can grow up free from any unconscious thoughts that they must adhere to someone else's rules simply because those rules represent the status quo. By this, I'm not suggesting we treat our toddlers like little adults. But it does mean that we afford them a sense of agency at a young age that increases as they mature. While I'm far from an expert on parenting and can only offer our experience, we have sought to make a move away from teaching our children *how* to behave and *what* to believe toward teaching them how to think and how to discern. We are paying more attention to shaping their values and ethics than simply insisting that they shouldn't (as my Pentecostal roots taught me) "smoke, chew, or run with the ones who do."

This means involving them in decision making processes (as appropriate for their age) to speak their mind, share their opinion, and talk about any reservations or concerns they may have. Truth be told, my six-year-old doesn't often contribute a whole lot of value right now to the decision making process of our family. But that's not the point. I also watch her eyes light up when she realizes she has a welcomed voice at our family table. It's a form of apprenticing whereby she can feel heard and understand that her voice contributes to our family. As Pentecostals, we are teaching them, little by little, how to hear the voice of the Holy Spirit, trust their discernment when they sense something is off, and learn to engage in age-appropriate spiritual warfare (e.g., learning to pray against fear as they fall asleep).

Egalitarian household codes prioritize healthy communication between family members, peace and harmony in the home, mutual respect and healthy boundaries, mutual understanding and shared responsibilities, healthy development, and psychological and emotional health for each member of the family. This means that each member of our family possesses the right to call a family meeting where they can air a grievance, even when that grievance is direct toward Tara or myself. We dialogue about it and seek to come to a resolution that promotes the peace of God and the unity of our family. We have made tending to the *shalom* of our home a key priority and breaching it (no matter if it is the children or us) a top problem to resolve.[5] Tara and I have attempted to eliminate the "because I said so" response from our vocabulary and actually give our children responses—even when the sheer volume of their questions feels like an impossible mountain to summit!

The goal that we've set out to walk out faithfully as a family is that, as our children age, we will slowly but surely adjust our relational dynamic with them so that by the time they reach adulthood, we are functioning as parental guides providing support and wisdom but not attempting to control or dominate, as we have witnessed parents of adult children doing. It is our hope that we will have invested our years with them in the home to cultivate godly wisdom and virtue, to help them see the world through the ethics of the kingdom of God and hear the still, small voice of the Spirit guiding them into adulthood.

Navigating Marital Disagreement

Hands down the most frequent question I get when I talk about co-leading the home with Tara is "who makes the final decision when you disagree?" Some insist that it is in these moments that the husband steps in as a sort of *primus inter pares* ("first among equals") to make the tiebreaking vote (I call this the "tiebreaker rule"), like the Vice President of the United States casting a tiebreaking vote in an equally divided Senate. But in reality, the question of who makes the final decision in a disagreement is the wrong question. The better question is, "how do you cultivate a relational intimacy strong enough where you can lead together by consensus?" In speaking with

---

5. By *shalom*, I don't simply mean peace, as the word is often translated from Scripture. Biblically *shalom* refers to a state of completeness and wholeness; that all is as it has been designed to be.

couples who have walked out egalitarian marriages with their spouse over multiple decades, most have actually never come to place where such a tie-breaker rule was necessary.

Discerning together as a couple requires a degree of patience so that, when there is not consensus, you talk it over and pray and talk it over some more and pray some more, until you come to a consensus. If you have a "nuclear option" like the tiebreaker rule, then equality is only an illusion. At the writing of this book, Tara and I have been married for fifteen years and, while there have been times early on where I wrongly insisted upon a particular decision thereby depriving her of decision making agency, as we have learned to better walk together as covenantal equals, the need for someone to have a final say has completely vanished. We simply do not move forward until we have agreement. And once we have agreement, the decision is equally hers as it is mine—equally mine as it is hers. It is *our* decision, for which we equally share the consequences.

Now, that does not mean we never defer to one another. While Tara and I are very similar in some respects, we both possess very different talents, strengths, and skills. So in our decision making, we weigh each of our opinions (and may defer to the other, consequently) through several criterion. Some include:

- **Who knows more?** Whose experience or education better qualifies them to speak to the issue with expertise? (Men: this requires that we don't presume we're an expert on everything!)

- **Who is thinking more clearly?** Depending on the season of life or the circumstances through which each of us are walking, who has the most rational head in this situation?

- **Who seems to have the greatest clarity from the Spirit?** Which of the two of us seems to have the mind of God more in the decision? Which decision best contributes to the wholeness of the family, the unity of the body of Christ, and the gospel witness to the broader community?

- **Who cares more?** Sometimes one of us cares far more about a situation than the other. And sometimes that's all that matters. Ultimately, I don't care what kind of knobs we put on our kitchen cabinets, but Tara does—so there's little reason for me to need equal say in the matter.

- **Who needs to crucify their flesh?** Whose pride, insecurity, or other fleshly impulses are driving their decision? Are both parties genuinely seeking the best for the other and for the family or does someone need to realign with the Holy Spirit?

Typically (though not exclusively) in our marriage, Tara has deferred to me when it concerns issues of safety. I have learned to defer to her on discerning how to handle relational situations with other people that require a great deal of wisdom. However, that is specific to our marriage. Yours might (and probably should) look different.

A VISION FOR EGALITARIAN MARRIAGE

In his *Treatises on Marriage*, the second century church father from Carthage, Tertullian, offers this vision for the ideal Christian marriage—one where women and men lead together as equals:

> How beautiful, then, the marriage of two Christians, two who are one in hope, one in desire, one in the way of life they follow, one in the religion they practice. They are as brother and sister, both servants of the same Master. Nothing divides them, either in flesh or in spirit. They are, in very truth, two in one flesh; and where there is but one flesh there is also but one spirit.
>
> They pray together, they worship together, they fast together; instructing one another, encouraging one another, strengthening one another. Side by side they visit God's church and partake of God's Banquet; side by side they face difficulties and persecution, share their consolations. They have no secrets from one another; they never shun each other's company; they never bring sorrow to each other's hearts. Unembarrassed they visit the sick and assist the needy.
>
> They give alms without anxiety; they attend the Sacrifice without difficulty; they perform their daily exercises of piety without hindrance. They need not be furtive about making the Sign of the Cross, nor timorous in greeting the brethren, nor silent in asking a blessing of God. Psalms and hymns they sing to one another, striving to see which one of them will chant more beautifully the praises of their Lord. Hearing and seeing this, Christ rejoices. To such as these He gives His peace. Where there are two together, there also He is present; and where He is, there evil is not.[6]

Here, Tertullian paints a very different picture than that which is often presented in the pro-patriarchy camp. He describes a marriage of mutual submission, mutual ministry, and mutual love for one another. This is the

---

6. *Treatise on Marriage*, 35–36, as quoted in Mowczko, "Tertullian on Equality and Mutuality in Marriage."

foundation of a healthy home that cultivates wholeness in the name of Jesus without using force, coercion, or Babel power to insist on having its own way (cf. 1 Cor 13:5 ESV).

Much of the concern I've seen expressed from folks who insist upon a male headship in the home is that without male headship the family is prone to spiritual waywardness, or the wife to rebellion. Someone once accused me of simply being too weak to make the decisions like "a real man." But co-leading alongside my wife has deepened our spiritual interdependence and thereby our spiritual intimacy with one another. We pray for each other. We sit and talk into the late hours of the night, discerning together. It has enriched the covenantal bonds between us. Make no mistake—it's not perfect! We both make poor decisions that temporarily destabilize the harmony of this approach to marriage and family. But most people who have led together in egalitarian marriages for a long time will tell you how wonderfully it enriches the bonds between both parties.

As for the "rebellion" of one's wife, when men and women move beyond the mental framework of *rulership* over a home into one of *stewardship*, the idea of a "rebelling wife" becomes absurd. It is a reminiscent holdover of the ancient assumptions that women were ontologically inferior to men and required a sort of parental hand similar to the children the husband and wife share. Often what is meant by a woman's "rebellion" looks less like Gomer's waywardness with Hosea and more like a woman who is tired of making sandwiches on demand and not having enough help around the house. A woman who insists upon her place as a functional equal in the home is not the sound of rebellion. It's the sound of freedom.

CHAPTER 7

Sex Begins in the Garden

EACH YEAR THROUGHOUT MY childhood, our family of five would pack up and drive from our home in Flint, Michigan to my grandparents' home in the rural countryside of west Georgia. Despite not having the modern parental crutches of iPads loaded with every Disney movie imaginable or the PBS Kids app, my parents did a pretty good job of keeping us occupied on the twelve-hour excursion down I-75. It was the only time we ever stopped for breakfast at McDonalds, for which I was a major fan. My mother would periodically take out little games, coloring books, and more that she'd picked up at the dollar store, arresting our attention for another couple hours. While my brother, sister, and I were preoccupied with those little goodies, she would read to my dad while he was driving. I vividly remember her working through Benny Hinn's classic *He Touched Me* and Tommy Tenney's *The God Chasers*.

Another book, of whose contents I have no recollection but whose title has been seared into the deepest recesses of my brain, is Christian psychologist Kevin Leman's work *Sex Begins in the Kitchen Because There's Company in the Living Room*. The book has been republished several times since its first publication in 1981 and has subsequently dropped the subtitle that I simply couldn't get past as a pre-teen boy. Why are mom and dad reading a book about having sex in the kitchen while people are over? Our house isn't even that big!

While I don't remember anything discussed in Leman's book, and I would probably have chosen a less traumatizing title, the phrase is forever etched into my psyche. But the sentiment of the title *does* ring true. Sex begins in the kitchen. Also in the car, on the phone, on the couch, and everywhere else you can imagine. By this, I refer to the intimacy that is cultivated between a husband and wife that often leads to sexual intercourse. Sex begins in the brain long before it leads to the bedroom.

Sex is wonderful. It can enhance the flourishing of a marriage in ways that few other things can. It is a gift from God for spouses to enjoy with one another and is itself a symbolic seal to ratify the covenant they share. But there is a great deal more about it than the act of physical intercourse that we (men, in particular) often overlook. For evangelicals, our bookshelves have been flooded over the past thirty-five years from popular level authors that have attempted to outline best practices in marriage, help couples understand one another, and more than a few go into explicit detail about the act of coitus itself.

One of the difficulties in the Christian marriage and sexuality industry is that it pervaded with underlying patriarchal themes and undertones. Christian marriage and sexuality author Sheila Wray Gregoire, who has written numerous books including *The Great Sex Rescue* and who blogs, podcasts, and develops scores of resources at her website Bare Marriage, has devoted countless hours to identifying the underlying patriarchal leanings in popular level marriage material. Rather than attempt to redo her fine work myself, I will simply recommend you to her. But Gregoire has taken a great deal of heat for highlighting that within the pages of marriage help books there is actually a great deal that is very unhelpful, especially for women. For instance, Gregoire points out, in her own chapter named "Sex Sorta Begins in the Kitchen (But Not Why You Think)" in *The Good Guy's Guide to Great Sex*, that men have been taught that if we do dishes or other forms of housework, our wives will want more sex. So if you want sex, then get to the kitchen sink . . . after all, sex begins in the kitchen! But Gregoire points out,

> This message of "Do X so she'll do Y" is pretty widespread. But when it's presented this way—*What can I do to make you want sex?*—then the emphasis is in the wrong place, and it can backfire bigtime . . .
>
> . . . If you compliment her on her looks as a ploy to get sex, she'll never really believe you think she's pretty. If you help around the house because you hope to get sex, she'll be left feeling that you actually expect her to do all the housework. If you do things with the expectation that you will get sex, you paint those acts of service as something she should be grateful for, as if you're

going the extra mile of acting like a true partner in the marriage. Kindness isn't kindness if you're doing it to get something. It's manipulation.[1]

You can see where resources that simply zero in on this dynamic, that men need to do more around the house or be more attentive in order for their wives to want sex can feel frustrating to men—especially when the underlying assumption that coincides with that is that, in doing the housework, the man is entering his wife's domain. He is "helping her." But that idea that he is helping her in the kitchen only makes sense if there is an underlying patriarchy present that assumes the kitchen is her duty to maintain. Because egalitarians have been fed patriarchal best practices in the home for decades, we have generally not even been well-exposed to what an egalitarian home might look like.

EQUAL IN THE CHURCH AND IN THE HOME

At present I want to offer a couple mindset shifts to consider as it pertains to fostering an environment of equality between men and women in the home. Because I just brought up Gregoire's passage about housework, I'll start there.

The Kitchen Can Be a Man's Domain, Too

Gregoire addresses that when men hear phrases like "sex begins in the kitchen" and the underlying instruction to do more housework to get more sex, our "Do X so she'll do Y" logical brains kick in. We tend to be sequential thinkers, thinkers who assume if we input one thing, we should expect an output of something else. If I put a dollar in a vending machine and select the right alphanumeric selection, a bottle of Pepsi or a bag of Doritos will come out. If I do the dishes, my wife will want to stop whatever she's doing to make passionate love to me.

But there are a couple reasons why this is wrong. The first, as Gregoire points out, is that it is manipulative. The motivation is not to add value to the home or make her life easier, but it is to do something in the hopes of activating her libido, so we get what we want. The second reason this is a wrong mindset though, as I noted in the previous section, is that the underlying assumption is patriarchal. If I'm "doing my wife a favor" by doing the dishes, I'm assuming that the dishes are her domain and I'm stepping in to

---

1. Gregoire and Gregoire, *Good Guy's Guide to Great Sex*, 100–101.

do a lift. While that's still normative for many households, it is a holdover from a period in American culture where women did not work outside of the home and were expected to be the caretakers of the home while the men "brought home the bacon." But, much to the chagrin of some men, we no longer live in such a society. Most families *need* an income from both spouses in order to make ends meet. Yet women continue to be expected, in one way or another, to hold down the fort when it comes to cooking and cleaning.

As I've noted previously, Tara and I have worked hard to make that shift mentally and functionally. While I brought the mindset into our marriage that I just described, we quickly began to realize how little that worked for us. But one of the biggest problems we had in dividing out kitchen responsibilities more equally was that, while I'm an excellent baker, I am not really a great cook (though I'm great with a grill). But if we wanted to eat *well* early in our marriage Tara had to be the one to cook. She will tell you that it was *very* difficult early on for me to set aside my ego to let her teach me some best practices in the kitchen. I was insecure about my lack of culinary prowess and the last thing I wanted was my wife to point that out. I confess, I can still get grumpy when I'm messing things up and I can tell she knows it, but I'm still a work in progress.

I started watching a lot of cooking videos, either on television or YouTube (Jacques Pépin's *Fast Food My Way* was especially helpful) to try to learn some fundamentals. But that takes time, so we made a rule between us that whoever did not cook was responsible for setting the table and for cleanup. That mostly fell on me because she did most of the cooking. But we had agreement, and both felt good about that rule.

I would be a liar if the old "sex begins in the kitchen" mentality didn't creep in occasionally. In my mind, I couldn't wrap my head around why Tara wasn't ready to just head upstairs after every time I turned that sink faucet off and beheld a clean kitchen after dinner. Afterall, I was *helping her out*. You can see how, even in a well-intentioned quest for sharing the load, I still unconsciously assumed I was doing her a favor.

Over time that fell away though (not without more than a few arguments!) and we share the burden of meal planning, preparation, and cleanup equally now. Attaining that equality has looked more like establishing a rhythm than establishing a balance. As with most things in life, if you strive for a perfect balance you'll wind up discouraged and disillusioned. If you strive for rhythm, you'll find yourself much more easily able to accommodate the ebbs and flows of life. Sometimes she does more of one or the other, sometimes that falls on me. As I'm writing these words, the night before I set the table and prepared a meal Tara had planned the week before and bought groceries for. When the meal was done we both instinctively just cleaned stuff up. The night before, however, I did everything—including cooking and cleaning. She had a long day at work and was exhausted and so I just stepped in and did "her" part (remember our "whoever doesn't cook cleans" rule) after having done mine to just let her relax. Believe me, there have been many nights where the opposite has happened as well.

What I've noticed is that over time my mentality had to shift from "I'm helping her out in the kitchen" to "it's *our* kitchen and we're in this together." This mentality of equality evolves from a contractual obligation that outlines what responsibilities belong to whom into this messy but beautiful rhythm of taking care of business together. What's more, sex is actually never even a part of the conversation of what happens in the kitchen, though what happens in the kitchen more greatly contributes to sex. More on that later.

Man Buns and Baby Björns

Another area men are told women go wild over is a man who is involved with his children. There's certainly some truth to that! As a teenager, a friend of mine and I would often babysit the infant son of one of the pastors at our church. We would frequently head to the local shopping mall with that little nugget in tow because girls were drawn to him like moths to a flame (of course, we were too terrified of girls to talk much to them, but we enjoyed the attention nevertheless). In past generations it was normative for fathers to be aloof and distant with their children, desiring for them to be seen but not heard. Now, however, the involved millennial father with his man bun drawn back and child strapped to his chest in a Baby Björn is *en vogue*.

This is undoubtedly a good change. While man buns may come and go, the Baby Björn-equipped father should be around to stay. Men have been told that their wives are attracted to a sensitive and available posture toward their children, and that's true. But there remains an underlying assumption, like the kitchen, that a man is doing woman's work by being with his children. I've heard, and you probably have too, people accidentally refer to fathers watching their children while their wives are out as "babysitting." I've heard men say it themselves! "Sorry, bro I can't go. I have to babysit the kids 'cause my wife has something going on tonight." My dudes, let me be clear: you cannot *babysit* that for which you are both spiritually and legally responsible. That's just called parenting. But there remains an underlying patriarchal assumption that an involved father is like a rare bird and that we should gaze upon the beauty of his child-rearing skills with wonder, lauding praises upon him for doing his part.

Being an elder millennial father, I've always been involved with our girls. The summer during which this book was written was one where I worked from home while our girls were on summer break so Tara could be in the office. Has it been easy? Hardly. But that's my role as a dad in this season. And while it has been said to Tara on more than one occasion how thankful she must be that I would be *willing* to do something like this, it's just a part of egalitarian parenting. There is an ebb and flow to equal parenting that is not always easy, but it works. And it works because both of us are able to be engaged outside of the home *and* be present with our children.

While Tara has said before that it warms her heart to watch me father our daughters (and the opposite when I'm grumpy), I'm not an involved father *so that* she will want to be physically intimate. That's not only manipulative, but it's also kind of gross. Men, be good and involved fathers for the sake of being good and involved fathers. Do it because your sons and your daughters need your emotional and physical availability to them. They need skin-to-skin contact as infants with their dads as much as they do their moms. They need to be hugged on and kissed on as little ones by dad as much as they do mom. Don't outsource the beautiful mess that is parenting to your wife. But also don't use involvement as a tool to try to manipulate your wife's libido.

Sex Begins in the Garden, Actually

While the sex begins in the kitchen schtick may be a helpful analogy for some, assuming the motivation is correct, there is perhaps a better one. How can I understand how to cultivate an intimate relationship with my wife that doesn't get reduced down to "Do X so she'll do Y" logic? It's tough. Men tend to prefer easy formulae. But I might suggest the garden analogy is better. *Sex begins in the garden.* By this I don't mean that if you spend time gardening, your wife will want to have sex. After all, fertilizer isn't exactly an aphrodisiac. But that is exactly why the analogy is better than the kitchen one. By "sex begins in the garden," I mean that stoking the fires of passion and intimacy in your marriage is more like tending to a garden than is the transactional nature of washing some dishes and expecting a reward.

Gardening is not a short-term activity. You plant seeds and water and fertilize and prune and spray for pests and all of the other things *knowing* that a harvest is fruit of that cultivating work—the beautiful fruit that comes from the hard work. But you cannot walk out one morning and plant some tomato seeds, only to come back that evening angry and frustrated that you don't have vine-ripened tomatoes waiting for you when you get home from work. That would be absurd! It takes time, gentleness, and patience. You cannot rush the cultivation of fruit—and truthfully you cannot even control the production of fruit. The plant bears fruit as a natural byproduct of a healthy environment, healthy soil, and good watering. As a gardener, your responsibility is not to yield fruit, but to tend carefully to the conditions necessary for the plants to do what they are created by God to do.

Sometimes external circumstances outside of a gardener's control delay or prohibit fruit from forming. When our family lived in Florida, we had a lemon tree in our backyard that blossomed beautifully. But once, a combination of pests and a brutal heatwave killed off those fragile buds, likely ruining my harvest from the tree for the season. Could I have preemptively sprayed for pests? Yes. But can I control prolonged heat? No. But is the tree worth cutting down and throwing away because I likely won't get fruit this season? Also no. Tending to the tree is more important than the fruit. And the next season, I was better prepared to defend my tree against threatening circumstances.

You're probably already picking up on my analogy here. The garden is your *marriage*, not your *spouse*. And together, husband and wife, you are co-laborers in your mutually-cultivated garden. When you patiently, consistently, and gently tend to your marriage, the marriage will naturally produce the fruit that it is formed by God to produce—which is a broader sexual intimacy that includes intercourse but is much deeper and more longsuffering than the physical act alone. But that takes patience, consistency, and gentleness. When the conditions of the soil are right and the plant is healthy, it will naturally bear good fruit. This does not mean that external hardships will not come—hardships that are either unforeseen or outside of your control. Job stress, a family loss, stress or conflict within your marriage, physical ailments, etc., can all inhibit the bearing of fruit. But it does mean that when those hardships come, you choose to value what you have grown and cultivated together, knowing on the other side of that hardship that fruit will begin to form again.

EQUALS IN THE BEDROOM

I vividly remember watching my parents tend to a garden in the backyard of my childhood home when I was growing up. I didn't understand gardening at all. All I observed was that both my mother and my father were out there religiously, doing this and that. Their respective duties seemed to be intertwined, one indistinguishable from the other. They tackled that garden year after year after year *together*. I never got the sense that the garden was my mother's job and my father was pitching in, or vice versa. It was their project that they tended to as equals.

This is how egalitarian marriages are cultivated. Women are not a sexual Rubik's cube men must maneuver and manipulate to unlock for their enjoyment. Neither is it solely a man's responsibility to tend to that environment so that a woman is sufficiently pleased. It's a joint effort to which both must commit and both must cultivate together. At face value, the outcome may be the bedroom, but the process of building shared intimacy with one another produces something far more beautiful and enduring than intercourse. It is this shared cultivation of intimacy that causes couples who have been married forty and fifty years to reflect upon how their sexual intimacy with one another is so much richer than it was in their twenties, despite the inevitable realities of aging.

One point of order that is central to why I chose to include this chapter to begin with, and to which I now must therefore turn, is the subject of consent and obligation. One of the harmful pieces of advice repeated over and over in all sorts of marriage books is that a woman is *obligated* to give sex to her husband, despite her being the "lesser libido spouse." Regardless of her wishes, she is responsible to satisfy the urges of her husband so that he is not led astray into pornography or extramarital affairs.

This is harmful for a couple of reasons. First, it continues to promote a prevailing assumption that in any relationship the woman is naturally the lesser-libido spouse. While this is sometimes the case, it is not always so. But promoting the notion that men always want sex and women never do forces those who do not fit that mold to internalize feelings of shame—as though a man is less of man if his wife is the higher libido spouse or that she is a sex-crazed maniac for possessing a higher sex drive than her husband.

The second reason this is harmful is because placing an obligation on one spouse to sexually perform for the sake of the other—especially when it is justified with "so they don't _____" (insert cheat, look at porn, etc.) deprives the individual (usually the woman) of agency and autonomy. She ceases to be a human person with boundaries to be respected and instead becomes an object to satisfy the physiological cravings of her spouse.

Some point to Paul's words in 1 Cor 7 as justification for the insistence of a wife's obligation to her husband to "put out":

> Now, about what you wrote: "It's good for a man not to have sex with a woman." Each man should have his own wife, and each woman should have her own husband because of sexual immorality. The husband should meet his wife's sexual needs, and the wife should do the same for her husband. The wife doesn't have

authority over her own body, but the husband does. Likewise, the husband doesn't have authority over his own body, but the wife does. Don't refuse to meet each other's needs unless you both agree for a short period of time to devote yourselves to prayer. Then come back together again so that Satan might not tempt you because of your lack of self-control. I'm saying this to give you permission; it's not a command. I wish all people were like me, but each has a particular gift from God: one has this gift, and another has that one. (1 Cor 7:1–7)

While there is indeed a call from Paul to make oneself available for one's spouse, there are a couple of points worth noting. First, Paul is not giving an arsenal to men to lord over their wives whenever they possess an urge. He is addressing both parties and calling both parties to recognize their *own* equal standing within the marriage bed. John Calvin noted of this verse:

> But it may be asked why the apostle here makes [husbands and wives] equal and does not demand obedience and subjection from the wife. I answer that it was not Paul's intention to discuss all their duties, but the mutual obligation that pertains to the marriage bed.[2]

Far from being a modern liberal feminist, Calvin points out that Paul's intention is to draw an equality between husband and wives and specifically not demand the subjection of the wife in the marriage bed. There is a mutuality which Paul is establishing here, not a trump card to play whenever one's spouse isn't in the mood.

The second point to note is that there are a some significant cultural dynamics happening behind the scenes of Paul's words to the Corinthians. Note that this section opens with Paul responding to questions the Christians in Corinth have brought to him (likely in a previous letter that has been lost to history). Among Greeks there was a common resistance to marriage, though sex was fine and all. Among Jews (and even some early Christians, in contrast to Paul), sex was considered only fine so long as it was for the procreation of children.[3] Some church fathers argued that sex even within the confines of marriage was sinful if it was only for recreational purposes.[4]

Paul's disciples in Corinth likely belonged to the second category who, despite being married, were remaining abstinent out of a desire to be pious

---

2. As quoted in Manetsch, *1 Corinthians*, 127.

3. Keener, *IVP Bible Background Commentary*, 473.

4. Manetsch, *1 Corinthians*, 124–25.

unto God.[5] So when Paul begins to treat the subject of abstinence in marriage he is not insisting upon any arbitrary frequency of intercourse between couples, nor is he weaponizing sex in the hands of one spouse against the other. He is essentially saying, "Look, it's great if you want to stay single. You can devote yourself solely to the Lord that way. But if you feel there's no way you could stay single, then get married! And if you're already married you need to abandon the idea that living a celibate life at the expense of your spouse is pleasing to God." That's a heavy paraphrase, but hopefully you get the point.

A second cultural dynamic at play here is the difference between our culture and that of the Christians in Corinth. In our culture, because we have been fed an assumption that men are these charged sex monsters and women must be coerced or manipulated into participating, we flip the script on which party, male or female, is primarily in view here. We read our own libido assumptions into the text: Paul's telling both men and women to make themselves available to each other, but he's *really* calling out the ladies. But the ancients would have likely seen the opposite. Jewish marriage contracts of the day stipulated that *man* must fulfill his duty to make himself available to his wife for intercourse.[6] Well into the nineteenth century it was women, not men, who were believed to be the more sexually charged gender. Beth Allison Barr points out that throughout medieval lore it is women who are portrayed as more prone to sexual sin and more likely to seduce a man than the other way around.[7] It is likely it was the married men in Corinth who were demanding abstinence out of a desire for personal piety, not women.

One final cultural dynamic is the subject of authority. Greek writers spoke of having sexual relations as coming under someone else's control or authority.[8] So when Paul is speaking of each exercising authority over the other's body, this is not license for the abuse of a spouse.[9] This resonates with Paul's words elsewhere (cf. Gal. 5:22–23; Phil 2:3) that call for mutuality and meekness in response to one another.

It would have been unthinkable for Paul for some to use his words, as they are sometimes used today, for a spouse to say to another, "your body belongs to me, so give it to me." Paul instead, is saying that because the husband and wife are in marriage for one another, they have come under

5. Keener, *IVP Bible Background Commentary*, 473; Barrett, *Commentary on the First Epistle to the Corinthians*, 156.

6. Keener, *IVP Bible Background Commentary*, 473.

7. Barr, *Making of Biblical Womanhood*, 86–87.

8. Keener, *IVP Bible Background Commentary*, 473.

9. Barrett, *Commentary on the First Epistle to the Corinthians*, 156.

the authority of the other in the way the Greek spoke of sex and authority. Paul applies that line of thought concerning fidelity in marriage. In other words, to seek sexual relations with someone outside of one's marriage was to "assert authority over their body against the matrimonial bond."[10] They're fused together like two metals—as Michael Scott would say in *The Office*: "Gold metals."[11] It is the Pauline version of Song of Songs 6:3: "I am my beloved's and my beloved is mine." The emphasis is on their covenantal submission to one another and the need to protect the sanctity of that covenant.

SEXUALITY BEYOND COITUS

I believe the image of tending a garden is helpful for both women and men but in particular for men. It helps us understand that there is a broader "sexual ecosystem" in our marriages than just sex itself. Sex is so much more than intercourse, just as gardening is so much more than harvesting ripened fruit. In his transformational book *The Deeply Formed Life*, Rich Villodas paints a picture of a human sexuality that is broader and more fulfilling than simple genital sex. Quoting Debra Hirsch, he establishes a definition for sexuality that is fundamentally a longing for deep connection and knowing before God and others.[12] That certainly involves coitus, but there is a broader social dimension to sexuality that we often miss. Speaking of a healthy and full sexuality in the image of a banquet, Villodas says,

> With the banquet diet, we are reminded that from the very beginning, humanity was made for community and intimacy with each other. We have often misplaced our longings and reaped the consequences, yet the offer remains. The sexual desires we possess, when ordered rightly, bring us to union with God and communion with each other. The love of God doesn't remove our desires; it reorders them.
>
> The banquet is the recognition that we were created for ecstasy but that this ecstasy is only found in God. He is the ultimate source of our lives, joy, and sexual desires. The starting point and the end point of our desires is God. This is the work of good theology and spiritual formation—believing that our bodies and sexuality were meant to point to something outside ourselves.[13]

10. Manetsch, *1 Corinthians*, 126–27.
11. *The Office*, "Phyllis' Wedding."
12. Villodas, *Deeply Formed Life*, 109–10.
13. Villodas, *Deeply Formed Life*, 117–18.

So if sexuality is more expansive than coitus alone, and there is a broader sexual ecosystem at play, what is it? Gregoire suggests a helpful framework for men to consider when attempting to cultivate the various dynamics of a sexual ecosystem. I believe that framework is helpful for men and women alike:

1. Emotional health

2. Physical health

3. Relational security

4. Emotional connection

5. Physically satisfying sex[14]

Gregoire suggests that if these five factors are present, they will lead to both parties desiring (genital) sex. I agree that this is true, in particular when those factors are cultivated over the course of time with consistency (an important caveat for men to recognize, I believe). But I also believe that the first four are also actually characteristics of a broader ecosystem of social sexuality that is not relegated only to married couples. In American culture we have lost sight of the deep and historical foundation of social sexuality— deep and meaningful friendships that are rooted in enduring trust, transparency, and security—that genital sex is intended to be built upon within a marriage. This is why a crucial, yet often overlooked, bedrock of enduring marriages are enduring friendships. Good *eros* is preceded by good *philia*. This has been a foundational truth that the ancients understood but one of which we have largely lost sight in American culture.[15]

For women and men to capture a sense of what a healthy and flourishing egalitarian marriage is, we must look to the image of a garden tended by both parties. But part of the outcome of the marital garden is in the process of tending to the garden itself. Gardeners don't become gardeners by picking fruit. Anyone with the ability to drive to a farmer's market or grocery store can do that. It is in the process of gardening that gardeners *become* gardeners, learning the tricks of the trade to keep healthy plants in good, healthy soil, so that they will yield good fruit in due season. The same is true of the marriage garden. The fruit of genital sexuality is best cultivated by two co-laborers in their marital garden who, together, learn how to build an ecosystem of flourishing social sexuality in their marriage—where each of them are fully known to each other and before God.

<hr>

14. Gregoire, "15 Things That Kill a Woman's Libido."

15. Yeh, "'Give Us Friends!'"

TEAR YOUR EYES OUT, BOYS

One final note on this subject of sexuality that I would be remiss to leave unaddressed in this chapter is about lust and our responsibility to prevent it. Allow me to illustrate with a story about a worship pastor named Amanda. Amanda and her husband Jake were both on staff as pastors at a mid-sized egalitarian church. She served as the worship pastor and he as the youth adult pastor. During their first year on staff at this church, Amanda became pregnant with their first child. Amanda grew up in a small, conservative town with very strict evangelical parents who stressed the importance of modest dress. So as Amanda's body began to change with the growing baby, she was very self-conscious about striking a good balance between dressing modestly without embracing the frumpy pregnancy styles of her mother in the 1980s. So, when the lead pastor's wife began to pull Amanda aside to chastise her about her appearance, Amanda was at a loss. The size of her breasts were a particular point of contention for this pastor's wife (who was, herself, subtly communicating the wishes of the lead pastor). In keeping with the universal biological reality that a woman's breast size increases during pregnancy, Amanda had the nerve to have grown her breasts *too* large, in the eyes of her pastors. This was a concern because it could potentially cause men to stumble in the service. No matter what outfit she wore, it never seemed to appease the peanut gallery. It was not until after their child was born and her breasts subsequently reduced in size again that the criticism stopped.

I've heard dozens of stories like Amanda's. You probably have heard them, too. They're not all the same, but they communicate the same basic principle: *women must dress modestly so men don't lust.* I've heard how the bodies of female clergy are assessed and analyzed by parishioners. I once was told by an adult woman how, as a young girl, she was made to swim at youth group events in a long sleeve turtleneck and a vest because her bust size was "inappropriately" large. I've heard stories of women accosted by men while they wore floor-length dresses, snowsuits, hooded sweatshirts, and more. I once even read how a female pastor in a mainline Protestant denomination was told how sexy she looked in her clerical robes. Even a cursory glance at news articles of sexual assault and abuse, both in and outside of the church, appear to demonstrate that a man's capacity to regulate his thoughts (and subsequent actions) has precious little to do with how much shoulder or kneecap a woman is showing. Yet the burden to prevent men from lusting somehow continues to fall upon women.

Scores of books have been written and thousands of youth group sermons have been preached to teach young men to avoid lusting after a woman and to teach young women to avoid being lusted after by a man. I vividly remember a well-meaning Sunday school teacher in my own youth, who told a classroom of pubescent boys about the "three-second rule"—that if you thought about a woman's beauty longer than three seconds it was lust, and lust was sin.

The basic, underlying premise isn't bad—lust *is* a sin—Jesus talks about it. In fact, Jesus talked about it in the Sermon on the Mount:

> But I say to you that every man who looks at a woman lustfully has already committed adultery in his heart. And if your right eye causes you to fall into sin, tear it out and throw it away. It's better that you lose a part of your body than that your whole body be thrown into hell. And if your right hand causes you to fall into sin, chop it off and throw it away. It's better that you lose a part of your body than that your whole body go into hell. (Matt 5:28–30)

But there are a couple key points worth considering. First, Jesus makes absolutely no mention of what the woman was doing, what she was wearing, whether she was out alone at night, whether or not she "had it comin'," or the scores of awful excuses we have all heard to explain away sexual impropriety toward women. One can reasonably deduce from Jesus' words that if a woman was stark naked in front of a man, it is *still* the man's responsibility to control himself in both thought and deed. There is no "she had it comin'" clause in Jesus' words to men about their responsibility to regulate their own thought lives. Jesus did not say, "And if your right hand causes you to fall into sin, chop it off and throw it away, *unless she's wearing a spaghetti strap tank top, boys, amirite?*" That sounds sacrilegious to even suggest yet modern evangelical purity culture functionally treats the words of Jesus this way.

In her book *Talking Back to Purity Culture*, Rachel Joy Welcher says this,

> I will never forget the day, during my time teaching at a private Christian high school, that a group of my female students gathered around my desk with furrowed brows and a flood of questions after having been told by another teacher: "You are responsible for the purity of men." It was picture day, so the girls were not wearing their uniforms but rather dresses and skirts that made them feel beautiful. Some of their skirts were shorter than usual, and this had prompted a gender-segregated speech on modesty by my coworker. Instead of feeling empowered by the idea that their dress had such influence over their male

classmates, their shoulders slumped under the weight of the responsibility placed on them.[16]

I've seen this in my own acquaintances—godly women who are *anything* but "on the prowl" looking to make men stumble—preoccupied on a daily basis with the task of making sure their outfits meet the unspoken, but ever shifting, expectations of a Christian culture that places the responsibility of male purity on women rather than upon men as Jesus explicitly did. Nearly every Sunday as we get ready to worship with our church, Tara engages me in a conversation about the appropriateness of her outfit, despite the fact that I've never seen her wear anything that could reasonably be considered inappropriate to church. But the conversation still happens because the psychological pressure placed upon young Christian women from purity culture is not easily exorcised.

The "women, you are responsible for the purity of men" message heaps loads of undue psychological shame upon Christian women—many of whom are already doing the best they can to be modest. As Welcher says, ". . . at some point the rhetoric of modesty begins to feel less about being wise and selfless and more about the sin of having a female body."[17] It sets an impossible standard, as ill-defined in its structure as steam, to set women up to feel that their bodies are a curse instead of a gift from the Lord. This is nothing more than another way to objectify women. Her body becomes something to be viewed as a potential threat that must be covered, like burying nuclear material deep into the ground to avoid it leaking into the atmosphere. When we zero so intently on the some*thing* of the female body, we lose sight of the some*one* of which that body is a part.

Men, let me be as clear as possible: *we*, not the women around us, are responsible for our thought life. Whether or not we lust is *our* responsibility, not theirs. While men need to hear that clear and biblical message, women do too. Some of the fiercest criticisms about the alleged immodesty of a woman often comes from other women. But whether the criticisms of modesty come from men or other women is no matter, it is of no matter. Be free in Jesus' name.

The other feature of Jesus' teaching is the object of his address itself: lust. Christian men, especially those of us who have come up under purity culture, have been taught to vigorously avoid lust at all costs. As a teenager, being in the presence of an attractive girl wasn't always easy. I was supposed to treat her like a daughter of God, but if my mind slipped toward appreciating something even as benign as how she looked that day, I was in danger of

16. Welcher, *Talking Back to Purity Culture*, 42–43.

17. Welcher, *Talking Back to Purity Culture*, 44.

the fires of hell. That's a bit of an overexaggerating, but for a church kid with approval issues, it wasn't far from the truth.

"Lust" is a word that is so frequently thrown around in Christian circles, its meaning is reduced to oblivion. Like other common words in the Christian lexicon such as "grace" and "faith," the definition of lust remains elusive, and therefore open to situational definitions that fit the needs of the moment. But lust does indeed have a legitimate framework that, if more men knew about, they would actually probably feel much less condemnation or fear of trespassing at lust's door than they do at present.

In his book *Money, Sex, and Power*, Richard Foster provides helpful insight on the subject of lust. Lust, says Foster,

> . . . produces bad sex, because it denies relationship. Lust turns the other person into an object, a thing, a nonperson. Jesus condemned lust because it cheapened sex, it made sex less than it was created to be. For Jesus, sex was too good, too high, too holy, to be thrown away by cheap thoughts.[18]

For Foster, lust is not noticing a member of the opposite sex, or even noticing that they're attractive. It is a "runaway, uncontrolled sexual passion" that objectifies the other.[19] In this regard, the heavy yoke we have put around women by shaming them for their female form as they have improperly born the weight of responsibility for the thought lives of their male counterparts trespasses on the sort of objectification in view by Foster more than observing that a woman is beautiful.[20] Quoting Lewis Smedes, Foster describes lust further:

> When the sense of excitement conceives a plan to use a person, when attraction turns into scheme, we have crossed beyond erotic excitement into spiritual adultery." Lust is an untamed inordinate sexual passion to possess, and this is a very different thing from the usual erotic awareness experienced in sexual fantasy.[21]

For many of us who were brought up with teachings such as the "three-second rule" I mentioned earlier, this is a vastly more liberating view of what lust is. It is also a high and holy call, not to count seconds or avoid eye contact, but to deeply behold our sisters in Christ as beloved sisters. To see them as genuine persons worthy of our respect and admiration and to take up the

---

18. Foster, *Money, Sex, and Power*, 99.

19. Foster, *Money, Sex, and Power*, 121.

20. Foster, *Money, Sex, and Power*, 105.

21. Foster, *Money, Sex, and Power*, 121., quoting Lewis Smedes, *Sex For Christians*, 130.

high calling to abhor objectifying them, either through "runaway, uncontrolled sexual passion" or through treating them and their bodies as objects to be feared and avoided. Runaway sexual passion and fearful avoidance are two sides of the same objectifying coin, and both should be rejected.

This topic of lust and the responsibility to avoid it is critical in empowering women in Christian community because this very topic lies at the heart of so much dysfunction between the sexes in Christian community. Pastors often will avoid mentoring or development conversations with staff of the opposite sex due to an inherent fear that finds its roots in this core issue. But if the issue at hand is depersonalization and objectification (whether it be lust-filled or avoidant), the remedy must rightly be the opposite—personalization and communion. It is entirely possible, and incredibly fulfilling to have genuine and meaningful friendships with members of the opposite gender without sex randomly combusting like holding a match to gasoline. Is accountability wise? Absolutely. But objectification through avoidance is no more the answer than unbridled passion. Learning to cultivate respect and honor for our sisters while taking back the biblical onus as it pertains to the condition of our own hearts—that's the answer.

Chapter 8

Invited to the Table . . .
So Long as She's Quiet

HAVE YOU EVER SAT in a meeting and suddenly realized that your physical presence was the only reason you were invited? I've been there a few times. I remember once being invited to strategic planning meeting for a parachurch organization I worked for. It was supposed to be a "meeting of the minds" that would help articulate the vision of the organization, how it would communicate its purpose to outsiders (including potential clients), and in no small way establish a blueprint for its future.

Now, I'm *very* good with strategic planning. There are many things I'm not good at, but organizational planning and vision articulation are very niche skills that I've developed, both through experience and in education. I also love doing it. So it was with this knowledge and a nerdy dose of excitement that I showed up to the swanky rooftop restaurant where we were to have this meeting, only to realize the meeting was already in full swing. I checked my phone to make sure I was on time and realized I *was* on time and that *wasn't* the meeting I was scheduled to attend, but rather a "meeting before the meeting" between only two key leaders and the organizational head.

When the actual meeting began and everyone sat down, one of the leaders who attended the pre-meeting spelled out everything they agreed upon in the pre-meeting. It immediately put a constraint upon the creative flow—because who wants to contradict your boss? But, being a little dense and not realizing yet what was happening, I spoke up anyway. I made some suggestions from some ideas that I had prepared before the meeting took place, though they differed from the conclusions of the pre-meeting. I still can feel the cool breeze that rushed through the group as silence ensued and I quickly realized, "Oh, this isn't one of *those* meetings. This is an agree and affirm your bosses' ideas sort of meeting."

You see, I was welcomed to the table so long as I kept quiet.

But why do organizations (even churches!) do this? At face value it seems to be a tremendous barrier to creativity and to organizational morale. And indeed it is! But I don't believe that most leaders consciously desire to inhibit creativity in their teams. Most leaders want more of that. I also don't believe most leaders want to damage morale. Everybody wants more of that, too.

But what I do believe is that it goes back to the Babel power I described in an earlier chapter, one that is rooted in insecurity. Leaders will often establish a baseline of control and invite others in to give an appearance of feedback, but without a genuine equality that allows feedback to flourish. It can be as serious and sinful as an abusive leader who implicitly demands a culture where those who work for him or her (though, most often him[1]) give only affirming feedback. There is a lot of that in churches, as Laura Barringer and Scot McKnight describe in their excellent work on healthy and unhealthy church cultures, *A Church Called Tov*.[2]

But leaders don't have to be narcissistic-leaning abusers to silence people at the table of ideas. Inexperienced or unskilled leaders who walk into a brainstorming meeting where they genuinely want to hear ideas often feel the need to lead out in the conversation. They will begin with something like, "Ok, so we're here to talk about [topic of discussion] today. I was thinking [gives his or her own opinions], but what do you all think?" That sounds benign enough, but it immediately establishes a baseline where the next person who speaks is forced to either affirm the leader's opinion (whether or not they agree) or appear adversarial to that opinion by suggesting something else. Experienced, collaborative leaders instead wait to give their opinion until a discussion is in full swing and there is an established cohesion in the meeting.

In other situations, leaders may invite people to the table of ideas, unconsciously seeking the *image* of agreement more than *actual* agreement. By this I mean that some leaders only want the stamp of approval from key stakeholders on an idea that is already theirs. These stampers may be an

---

1. McKnight and Barringer, *Church Called Tov*, 47.

2. McKnight and Barringer, *Church Called Tov*, 39–51.

expert on a team, someone with significant political capital, a highly educated person, etc. Or they may be people of color and/or women.

Women encounter these sorts of "shut up, sit down, and look pretty" environments within organizational cultures often. Especially in modern American culture, where increased emphasis is being placed on diverse representation of people of color and women within organizational leadership structures. Organizations often respond by diversifying their staff, so if you were to take a group photo of their staff, it would have the *image* of empowerment without *actual* empowerment. I dare say that this is so common that if you were to sit in a room with a dozen random women who are employed in just about any organization, more than a few could share a story of being a part of an organization that had all of the appearance of diversity while denying its power by keeping those diverse voices from places where they can shape vision and strategy. This is due to the fact that many organizations, including churches, stop short by seeking only diversity. Let's take a moment and explore that idea.

DIVERSITY, EQUITY, INCLUSION

Diversity, equity, and inclusion (DEI) are related but separate concepts. There is a whole field of DEI studies and a whole workforce who speak into organizations with authority on the subject. But for the purposes of this chapter, I want to make it very simple to understand the differences between these concepts:

- Diversity is equal representation.
- Equity is equal opportunity.
- Inclusion is equal voice.

The University of Michigan's Chief Diversity Officer Robert Sellers' metaphor of attending a "DEI Dance" is very appropriate here:[3]

- Diversity is when everyone is invited to attend the party.
- Equity is when everyone gets the opportunity to dance.
- Inclusion is when everyone gets to contribute to the playlist.

Many organizations, including churches stop short of simply inviting women to the dance. They may even vigorously work to actively invite women to the dance. But if and when the women show up, they find

3. "Defining DEI."

themselves at a party that has been planned exclusively by men. The venue was chosen by men. The songs were chosen by men. The decorations were chosen by men. The party, at its core, is a guy's party to which women have shown up.

Among egalitarian churches, there are many that are a guy's party that women simply show up to. All too many churches have all the appearance of egalitarianism while denying its power. They have a thin candy-coated egalitarian shell that masks an internal organization that is otherwise patriarchal—a guy's party.

From Diversity to Equity

Moving from beyond diversity to equity means providing equal opportunity, not simply to attend the party but to be involved in all areas. No church or organization can be equitable toward women when it tells women they are not allowed to dance when certain songs come on or at certain times during the event. Equity is not allowing women to dance, so long as they are accompanied by their husbands or if it's a "gal's only" dance moment in an otherwise male dominated soirée. Likewise, true and biblical equity does not permit women to perform certain duties within a church while denying them others. Biblical equity does not permit women opportunity to *only* a certain level of authority in an organization solely because of their gender. Biblical equity does not "allow" her to lead, so long as it is alongside her husband or by leading other women.

Rather, a biblically faithful equity considers the calling, capacity, and character of a woman when making decisions about opportunity within the organization—by virtue of her daughterhood in the kingdom than the nature of her anatomy. Ultimately, a guy's party to which women are invited but prohibited from being a part of the planning inhibits the progress of the organization. Sandi, who I mentioned earlier, put it this way:

> Women are often given responsibilities within the church without being given authority. We have often heard it said that in ministry 20% of the people do 80% of the work. That's very true and it also seems like 80% of those people are women while women have at best 20% of the authority. Pastors need to realize how much this limits the impact of the church. They become the lid, the bottleneck to anything being done. Women are often ready willing and able to get things done but are standing around waiting on a pastor to tell them they are allowed.

From Equity to Inclusion

Moving beyond equity to inclusion is difficult for many organizations because it requires that the organization change to accommodate the diverse perspectives and input of women. The party ceases to look decidedly male-run and takes on a more feminine tone. That doesn't mean the church or organization *becomes* feminine, as some have decried the trajectory of the church to be headed. But it means that different voices are speaking into the playlist for the party.

Our family has been blessed to live in very diverse communities. Puerto Ricans, Colombians, Iraqis, and Indians all have been our next-door neighbors. But if I were to throw a community block party that *genuinely* reflected our community, would my Spotify playlist of 90s country music do the trick? It would be odd, inconsiderate even, to throw a party in the neighborhood that didn't solicit the input of the rich musical tastes that are represented in this beautifully diverse community. How foolish would I be to miss out on the opportunity to broaden my musical tastes beyond Alan Jackson and Rascal Flatts simply because I didn't want to give up control?

But in egalitarian spaces we often do precisely this. We will snap photos of women on our church stages, or even preaching on Mother's Day, and feel that we have satisfied the demands of diversity. But inclusion affords our churches the ability to hear the Spirit-filled feminine heart from the pulpit year-round. Inclusion cultivates belonging for women so that they feel that church is a space that is uniquely *theirs*, too. Inclusion requires giving up power. It requires intentionality. It requires a posture of listening.

The icky space between equity and inclusion is *tokenism*. Tokenism is when a woman (or any other minority in an organization) is elevated to a position or platformed for impure reasons. Those reasons may not be consciously nefarious, but they are impure nevertheless. Tokenism will elevate a woman to use her as an object rather than a source of authority. She may be the obligatory annual female preacher so that a church can say, "we let the women preach, too." She may be the lone executive on an otherwise all-male team that lacks the same degree of authority and power. Often women in token positions will be brought close to the center of power when it suits the powerful and then kept at arm's length at all other times. Token women exist in organizations that desire the appearance of inclusion in order to satisfy the demands of advocates for women. I recall several years ago speaking with a denominational official in an egalitarian denomination who pointed to a woman who was an administrator in their denomination's district office as proof that their leadership was doing a satisfactory job with empowering women (despite the fact that few churches in the district employed female pastors and the denominational district itself had no female lead pastors).

Organizations who leverage tokenism as a cover for underlying patriarchy can be spotted because when they are questioned about the absence of female empowerment, they will have at the ready one or two women they can point to and say, "Look! We're doing a good job with that." Organizations that seek genuine inclusion, even when they have much work to do, will instead acknowledge where gaps exist and invite *women* to speak to how those gaps can be remedied. Organizations, including churches, that are genuinely inclusive of women have an acute sense of how they are doing, not because they are pointing to the token women within their ranks, but because those women have the freedom to speak up (and are proactively invited to speak up), not only to how the organization should run but also to how it can better empower other women.

Tokenism is, at its core, abuse. Abuse does not need to be intentional to be abusive. But, as Wade Mullen says, "When someone treats you as an object they are willing to harm for their own benefit, abuse has occurred . . . abuse involves any action that takes power away from another in an attempt to use them."[4] Establishing an illusionary effect where a woman is platformed to give the appearance of power without the giving of that power is abuse. Promoting a woman into a position that carries only the responsibility of the role while depriving them of the authority to carry that position out—often without the intervention of a male colleague—is abuse. In my view, there's a way in which tokenism is worse than simply outright denying inclusion because it introduces a deceptive element that is harmful to women.

From Inclusion to Empowerment

While DEI specialists may include what I'm about to outline as a component of inclusion, I insist that a necessary and explicit step beyond inclusion is *empowerment*. While inclusion is inviting everyone to select the playlist for the dance, empowerment is inviting qualified representation to the party planning committee. Inclusion may set the tone of the party, but empowerment determines whether a party should even take place and, if so, when, where, and how it should be carried out. Inclusion may choose the playlist, but empowerment chooses the music streaming platform.

While the inclusion of women in an organization speaks to their sense of belonging within it and their voice being invited to speak into how things

4. Mullen, *Something's Not Right*, 2.

are carried out, empowerment speaks to, well, *power*. It matters less that a woman holds *a* role within an organization and more *what* roles they hold. When you think of the inner circle of power within your church or organization, are any women there? Is there more than just one there? And if women are present, to what extent do they hold position and not actually possess real power? After all, women will often be invited to have a seat at the table . . . so long as they're quiet.

As noted previously, I've used a secret little tool for quickly assessing the extent to which a church is empowering of its women. I look at the website, but I skip past the homepage, any vision pages, or descriptions of statements of belief. I go right to the staff page. Understanding a church's ethos can be difficult on a website, in particular as it pertains to the church's position on women. But looking at the church's staffing page allows me to move beyond the church's *stated* theology of women to its *lived* theology of women. I look to see first, if *any* women appear on the church's staff outside of administrative roles (often they do not). But then I look to see *what* roles those women fill. Many churches that claim an egalitarian theology have women on staff, but they all fill non-pastoral roles. A theologically-egalitarian church whose female staff are all directors, coordinators, administrators, and managers is a functionally-patriarchal church. Finally, if there are women on the pastoral staff, I look to see the extent to which women are represented within executive leadership. A church may functionally empower women as clergy, but when men alone are in the executive seats of authority that direct the vision, culture, and tone of the church, the church has yet to fully step into its call to empower its daughters to their fullest capacity.

What does empowerment look like for a church? I remember a conversation I had a couple years ago with a friend of mine, recording artist (and Harley Davidson aficionado) Paul Wilbur. I asked Wilbur, who has a deep passion to see Messianic Jewish and Gentile Christians foster relational reconciliation, what he envisioned of a church that truly was a "one new humanity" expression of Christianity (a term we used to refer to fully reconciled Jewish and Gentile believers, cf. Eph. 2:14–16). He responded that it would be something where both gentiles and Jewish believers could feel that the church bore their DNA. Each group's unique sound would be represented in worship. Each's unique calendrical celebrations would be honored. That each would defer to the other in love so that no one voice drowned out the other. That, at the church's core it would be both Jewish and Gentile in its DNA.

What Wilbur described, at its core, is empowerment. Between Jewish and gentile believers in the Messiah, empowerment means both parties are equally represented—not simply in stage time or in photos but that when someone walked in to the worship service or when someone visited a gathering of group of church members throughout the week, both Jewish and gentile believers alike would feel that their voice helped shaped what they saw.

Regarding gender, empowerment brings us to a place where women do not simply feel that they are invited to add value to an organization that is foundationally male, but that their unique feminine touch can shape the very nature of the organization. Some men are terrified of that. I believe the reasons for that terror can be past trauma (e.g., abusive or overbearing mothers), and it can also be ego or insecurity. We men have much more insecurity than we often care to admit. The masculinity of some men is as fragile as single-pane glass, ready to burst into a million pieces with the slightest degree of pressure. They assume that if women get to choose the playlists then they'll somehow end up wearing a dress and sitting down to a tea party, debating the versatility of Repose Gray as an interior paint color.

But men exhibiting real masculinity recognize that making room for women to help shape how the party is planned is not a threat to their masculinity. I've never felt more manly than when I get to watch my wife flourish in her calling. I've never felt like a better man than when I get to use my privileged gender to advocate for women in the churches and organizations in which I've served. Empowering women is not the pet hobby of a few men. It is the biblical duty of us all. It is how we participate with Christ in walking out the reversal of the curse of Gen 3.

DOUBLE CONSCIOUSNESS IN GENDER

In his excellent book *The Next Evangelicalism*, Soong-Chan Rah speaks about the issue of double and triple consciousness among ethnic minority groups in the United States. In his treatment, he quotes W. E. B. Du Bois's *The Souls of Black Folk:*

> It is a peculiar sensation, this double-consciousness, this sense of always looking at one's self through the eyes of others, of measuring one's soul by the tape of a world that looks on in amused contempt or pity. One ever feels his twoness—an American, a Negro; two souls, two thoughts, to unreconcilable strings.[5]

Du Bois's words illuminate how white people, men and women alike, experience a mono-consciousness in America. We are *American*. Wherever we go, there our singular consciousness as Americans takes us because we live

5. Du Bois, *Souls of Black Folk*, 215, as quoted in Rah, *Next Evangelicalism*, 182.

in a culture that has been formed by white society. African Americans, says Rah, "must deal with the reality of not being totally accepted in white society and having to behave in a certain manner in society at large, while behaving in another manner (maybe a more 'natural' manner) in their own cultural setting of the black community (i.e., the black neighborhood, church, etc.)."[6] He goes on to cite the work of Eldin Villafañe who broadened the application to second-generation Hispanics, who possess a "triple consciousness" (one among Anglo-Whites, a second among first-generation Hispanics, and a third among other second- and third-generation Hispanics).[7]

I want to be very careful to honor the uniqueness of the double and triple consciousness of ethnic minorities in my application of this concept to women in ministry. There is a very real sense in which white women enjoy a mono-consciousness by virtue of their race that is not enjoyed by women of color. It is, in so many respects, *not* the same.

There is, however, a very profound degree to which I have observed a degree of double consciousness among women in church ministry that is indeed worth noting. For the female pastor, there is an ever-present awareness that she occupies space in a vocation which has, for centuries, been dominated by men. It is a male-shaped space in ways that few other professions are. In that respect, women in ministry possess a double consciousness. She must be "on" in mixed company with other pastors who are men. She is keenly aware of how she must navigate the egos of her male colleagues in the room—so as to appear neither too compliant nor too domineering. She must navigate that duality of stepping into the pulpit while being conscious of her attire, lest (as I noted in the previous chapter) she get feedback from the modesty police. Female clergy are one hundred percent *clergy*, but they are also something else, too—they're *female* clergy. I've spoken with scores of female pastors in time in ministry, and I hear over and again how this double consciousness plays out. While they get on in mixed gender pastoral spaces just fine, there is another unique way of being when they are in a homogenous setting with other female pastors.

This is further compounded when we simply apply at face value what Rah, and before him Du Bois, have said about the experiences of people of color to women of color in pastoral spaces, especially when those spaces are dominated by white men. So while the white female pastor experiences the double consciousness of being a pastor and of being a female pastor, the female pastor of color experiences a triple consciousness: 1) being with pastors (mixed gender), 2) being with female pastors (mixed race), and 3)

6. Rah, *Next Evangelicalism*, 182.

7. Rah, *Next Evangelicalism*, 182.

being among female pastors (homogenous race). If the woman of color is a second-generation immigrant, such as the scenario Rah described above, this adds yet a fourth dimension still.

Why does this even matter? First, the multiple consciousness is not a bad thing; it's natural. But it can also be exacerbated by having to change how one engages with other groups due to unequal power dynamics or other forms of inequity. For instance, in a room full of mostly white and male clergy, a woman is going to naturally feel a need to be aware of the "temperature" of the egos in the room in order to get by (something to which men do not generally have to give much thought). By simply being aware that a woman, especially a woman of color, naturally feels different in a room with you because you're a male, that awareness can go a long way to determine how you treat her. You don't need to be condescending or awkward about those differences—being aware and intentional about listening is often half of the battle.

The second reason this matters is because, laden within this multiple consciousness, is tremendous potential for growth and learning for the whole body of Christ. Rah notes how multiple-conscious individuals provide common links that cross normal barriers like ethnicity. On this point, Rah says,

> Even if the details differ, the ethos and "feel" of those with a third culture or a triple consciousness are similar. For example, some of the best insights I have learned about ministry to Asian Americans have come from Hispanic American theologian Eldin Villafañe's writings and teachings on the second-generation Puerto-Rican American experience.[8]

Multiple-conscious people teach us about ourselves in ways we can never learn on our own. They are able to step outside of themselves in a way that those of us who are mono-conscious cannot. Some of the most profound insights I have learned as a pastor have come from female clergy, especially female clergy of color. They convict and inform me of my own pastoral theology and practice in a way that no other sort of relationship can do. Hear me when I tell you, if you want a truly empowering church that taps into the voices of and ministers to every demographic in your city, inviting the voices of women to the table and listening intently while they speak what the Spirit is speaking to and through them will profoundly and radically change the way you do ministry, for the good.

---

8. Rah, *Next Evangelicalism*, 187.

CHAPTER 9

Crabs in a Bucket

IN MANY MARKETS AROUND the world, you will find crabs for sale. Like lobster, crab are best when sold alive, so in many markets, when you find available crab, they're often just all chilling in an open bucket or basket.

Now crab are agile little creatures. They can maneuver about and, in certain circumstances, even climb. Some crab in the wild are known to take shelter in trees, even! But folks who sell crab in markets don't have to bother with putting a lid on the crab bucket. Why? Because the crabs keep each other in the bucket.

While the crabs are all trying to climb out of the bucket, the crab at the top always gets pulled down by the others. Another ascends, only to be subsequently sabotaged by his or her prison mates. No crabs escape because as one ascends to the highest heights, it is brought low again by those seeking to scramble to the top themselves. It's as though they say to the escaping crab, "If I can't have it, neither can you."[1]

The lesson we can learn from the crabs is that when we believe a resource is scarce, we can, if we're not careful, become like those crabs in a bucket: "If I can't have it, neither can you."

Among Christian women, I've often observed a crab-in-a-bucket mentality. And in speaking with numerous women who are in leadership in egalitarian spaces, it is often other *women*, not just men, who they cite as their biggest hurdles for advancement. As with power, which I talked about previously, opportunity can be perceived as a limited resource. There are

---

1. Low, *Good Intentions Are Not Enough*, 104.

only so many spots at the top of the mountain after all, right? And if men only grant women access to a few of those spots, *which* women get the spot becomes a point of contention. In her book, *The Language of Female Leadership*, Judith Baxter associates the scarcity of executive leadership positions within an organization with a diminished support from other women and the cultivation of an atmosphere of distrust.[2] When scarcity abounds, distrust and self-preservation are a significant temptation.

At present, I will outline a few ways in which Christian women in egalitarian spaces function as crabs in a bucket toward one another.

UNDERMINING THE SUCCESS OR AMBITION OF ANOTHER WOMAN

While it's neither godly nor desirable, it is normal to experience feelings of jealousy when someone who is similarly skilled and educated as you gets an opportunity or a promotion instead of you. But the crab in the bucket mentality is perhaps most evident when that subtle, momentary jealousy takes root and matures into an unhealthier form of resistance and sabotage to another person's success. This can include building relational coalitions within workplaces based on a mutual feeling of disdain for the target woman's success. It may include actively seeking to undermine her, to pull her down from reaching the top of the bucket, as it were. Because, after all, if you can't have the opportunity, neither should she!

One example is from the experience of Kelly, who pursued a traditionally male career field and, upon entering that field and achieving her dream, was told by women in the church where her husband pastored that she was going to "prevent him from fulfilling his call" because her career success would undermine her ability to be a supportive pastor's wife.

I remember a similar encounter at an engagement party that friends and family threw for Tara and me before our wedding. During the party, which was held at my home church, one of the wives of the pastors on staff laughingly explained to Tara why her ambition to seek out a pastoral role in ministry alongside me was silly because I would already carry the title of pastor.

In another instance, Erin, who worked as a staff pastor at a mid-sized egalitarian church, was promoted above some of her female coworkers at the church. She described to me how female staff began to rally and spread falsehoods about her, until her senior leadership had to step in and put a

---

2. Baxter, *Language of Female Leadership*, 170, as attributed in Morgan, "Best Practices For Developing Female Leaders In Egalitarian Churches," 67.

stop to it. "Some women would rather see a male in a ministry position than a woman, and they work to make that happen," she told me.[3]

Still another example came to me from a man, Jeff, who pastors an egalitarian church with two additional pastors on his staff—both women. He noted to me that while the men in his church are very supportive, his female staff have noted how they *do* receive opposition, and it is almost always from other women in the congregation. He attributes the resistance from the women of the house to patriarchal assumptions the women have brought into the church about male headship. His staff, in their view, are breaching that pattern of male headship (never mind, of course, that Jeff is the senior pastor!).

Undermining the success, the advancement, or even the *ambition* to achieve something is classic crab mentality. But as the crab illustration shows us, when women pull other women down who are trying to succeed or who have dreams or aspirations, everyone loses.

QUEEN BEE SYNDROME

Queen bee syndrome is a form of crab mentality but slightly different than the scenarios I just described. Rather than women (from "below" in the bucket) attempting to pull women down who are attempting to ascend higher, queen bee syndrome is when a woman who has achieved keeps other women down. It is the organizational equivalent of the classic scene in Disney's *The Lion King* where Scar, safely at the top of the cliff, digs his claws into a struggling Mufasa and pushes him to his demise rather than help him to safety.

Queen bee syndrome was a term coined by psychologists at the University of Michigan in the 1970s. Today, it is somewhat controversial among experts because it also makes other, outdated assumptions of masculine and feminine character traits (e.g., queen bees were assumed to adopt more masculine leadership traits to get ahead). But current studies, as well as much anecdotal evidence, suggest that on the whole women can find themselves in a more difficult position to succeed when the gatekeeper for that success is a woman.[4]

As I've observed in church settings, queen bee syndrome can manifest itself in several ways. Female queen bees may freeze other women out of stage roles or opportunities for fear that the rising female employee will steal the spotlight. Anna Morgan, academic dean at Ascent College and lead

3. Personal correspondence, Oct 6, 2022.
4. "Queen Bees."

pastor of Word of Life International Church in Alexandria, Virginia, did her doctoral research at Fuller Seminary on the development of female leaders. She identified the spotlight sharing as one of the most significant manifestations of queen bee syndrome:

> I observe [queen bee syndrome] in the church world most obviously in preaching opportunities. There are many, many opportunities for men to preach in churches. Far fewer opportunities exist for female preachers. So women are less likely to open doors for other women to preach, to pass along opportunities. Instead, the women with power take every opportunity that comes their way.
>
> This is true inside an egalitarian church, particularly when the senior pastor is male and does most of the preaching on Sundays, leaving just a handful of opportunities for a woman. It's also true of conferences/itinerate ministry. It's very hard for a woman to come by opportunities to develop her preaching gift, and even harder if there is another woman with more power who is also a preacher in her world.[5]

Some church bees who are well-established in their ministry careers may resent the difficult road they had to pioneer in a field long dominated by men. As such, they see the (relatively) smoother path of younger women in ministry to be something that can make them "soft" (this is not unlike the feelings many first-generation builders of wealth experience when handing off wealth to their children). Still other queen bees may simply enjoy being the lone female representation at executive levels.

One area queen bee syndrome is particularly pronounced is in the development of younger women. For women who are in positions of leadership, especially in churches, the presence of a more seasoned woman in the profession is a rare gift. Simply because most pastors, even in egalitarian churches, are men, women often must turn to veteran male pastors for professional development. But because of stigma surrounding mixed-gender mentorship and other developmentally inhibitive ministry practices, many women are left with minimal to no direct development or mentorship from their male pastoral superiors. This is a pain point that I hear brought up over and again from young female clergy. So, the presence of a veteran female pastor is a rare gift to them.

Except many queen bees do not desire or do not prioritize the development of younger females. In my time in ministry, I have worked with seasoned female pastors who expressed both sentiments. One, for example,

5. Personal correspondence, Oct 13, 2022.

expressed an intense desire to mentor younger women but simply did not have the time. Another expressed that it wasn't her responsibility to develop younger women and that if female staff desired that, they should look elsewhere.

Rather than coaching and mentorship, what many young female clergy find from their elder mothers in the faith is condescension and judgment. Cassidy, who is a licensed missionary with an egalitarian denomination and who has ministered on American college campuses for fifteen years recalled to me about a time she was attending a denominational event and had her two-year-old in tow. On the last day of a several-day conference, her toddler had just had enough and, as all two-year-olds do, she began to act up. Cassidy took her to the back of the room and gave her daughter her tablet to keep her occupied while she could continue listening to the final session of the conference. An older woman (who she did not know) approached Cassidy and berated her with belittling and sarcastic comments about Cassidy's mothering. Cassidy was so taken aback and hurt by the ordeal, she told me that what was, in the conference, supposed to be a time to encourage and strengthen her in ministry, turned into a spiral where she questioned everything about her calling for several days after. All because of the sting of a queen bee.

Seasoned female leaders in ministry must consider that the roads they have trailblazed will eventually become overgrown and unwalkable if they do not strengthen the position of the next generation of female pastors coming up behind them. The next generation of female leaders will either pave those trailblazed roads or they will be forced to cut back the weeds of overgrowth from years of developmental neglect. Much of that depends on how elder women in ministry choose to pour into the generation behind them. Young female clergy are starving for mentors, both women and men. We all need to meet that need.

Ironically, Morgan notes that for those women who have become "truly significant kingdom leaders" there is a much greater vision for the development, creation of opportunities, and sponsorship of up-and-coming female clergy.[6] This further illustrates the function of Passover power (chapter four). In the economy of the kingdom, when power is given away it multiplies. Could it be that there is a spiritual correlation between the posture of these women toward helping others and their elevated place in the church?

6. Personal correspondence, Oct 13, 2022.

MODESTY POLICING

Earlier I mentioned how women experience modesty policing in their ministries—that is others coming to her with (often conflicting) "advice" for how she should dress. As I've talked to women, I've been surprised to find that most often that modesty policing comes from *other* women rather than men. Men are often more covert in their judgments about female modesty, often hiding behind screens, pulpits, and at times even their wives to make their thoughts known, women can be brutal to their own when it comes to policing dress and appearance. Often some of the most confusing and contradictory directives from the "modesty police" that women receive come from other women.

Shannon, who is a children's pastor at an egalitarian church in her thirties described some of her run-ins with the modesty police:

> I've been told that I'm being immodest attending events or group meetings alone (unchaperoned), especially if I'm the only woman in attendance.
>
> I've been told only to wear dresses because I should hold on to my femininity (i.e., don't be too masculine). I've been told I should avoid dresses or skirts so as not to tempt my male ministry colleagues.
>
> I've been told I always need to wear makeup because it is what makes a woman appear professional. I've been told not to wear makeup because it makes me promiscuous.
>
> I've been told to "stick to female ministry areas" like women's ministry or kids ministry . . . I've been told to break the glass ceiling.[7]

Like the worship pastor who receives complaints that the music was too soft and that it was too loud on the same Sunday, women are levied contradictory and impossible standards of modesty and propriety and it is perpetuated most often by other women.

ADOPTING THE TURTLE MINDSET

Unlike crabs in a bucket who pull each other down, turtles handle each other in a completely different way. From the moment they hatch, turtles seem determined to work as a team. If you've ever watched turtles in a documentary, they're fascinating little creatures. Even with their limited range of

---

7. Personal correspondence, Oct 6, 2022.

motion, they help each other climb from their collective nest after hatching. When sea turtles make their break to the open waters, attempting to move fast lest they be picked off by a predator, they will actually push one another forward. You can even look up videos on online of turtles who rush to the aid of one of their comrades who has tipped upside-down. Lying stranded on his back with his stubby little legs moving about, neighboring turtles will position themselves to push their friend upright so he can carry on.

Applying that metaphor to collaboration in ministry and in organizations doesn't require much elaboration. Women navigate more pressures, struggles, and outright opposition in ministry and career than most of us men can fathom. In nearly two decades of ministry, I've witnessed with my own eyes, and heard from countless women, the pain that women inflict upon one another. But I've also seen women in ministry function like turtles instead of crabs. I've been in ministry settings where women were being discriminated against and banded together to demand representation and change and won it.

Never underestimate the effectiveness of women banded together for a common purpose. One need only look at the women's suffrage movement in the United States, wherein a group of dedicated women managed to convince an all-male electorate to give them their right to vote. A woman walking out her calling from the Lord is a powerful thing. But a group of women walking arm-in-arm, determined to support and champion one another in their respective callings . . . that's an unstoppable force.

Chapter 10

Women and the Future
of the Church

As you've made it nearly to the end of the journey through this book, it is my hope that you will walk away affirming a few basic truth claims, which I will outline in this final chapter. Early, when I was still pitching the idea of this book, someone's feedback to me was that it was "too academic for trade and too trade-y for academic." While this feedback was well-intentioned and normally is sound advice to heed, I felt deeply that this *via media* ("middle way") was exactly what this book needed to attain the purpose for which I set out to write it.

Namely, I wanted to write a book that bridged the gap between the excellent scholarship being done among egalitarian scholars and the broader Christian community. I hope to bridge that gap by providing something that is accessible to anyone who picks it up, while still being substantive enough as to provide both practical and theological insight from which anyone can benefit. I believe the future of the church depends on it. By this I don't mean that if you don't adopt what I've recommended the church won't survive. Hardly. The church marches on, enduring through time and across vast distances. It will continue to endure because the church is God's missionary people sent into the world, and God's reconciliatory mission, as revealed in the redemptive work of Jesus the Messiah, will not be complete until his return.

What I do mean when I say that the future of the church depends on learning to move beyond a passive supporter of Christian women to a passionate advocate, is that the church's capacity to flourish in the twenty-first century will depend in large part in how it stewards its sisters and daughters. If you look at nearly every great period of Christian renewal movement throughout history, you will find two things. First, on the surface you will see men. Men like Paul, Francis of Assisi, Martin Luther, John Wesley, and William Seymour. Men are generally who we've oriented the story around.

But the second thing you will find are dedicated women, often defying social and ecclesial expectations to be faithful to what God has called them to do. Women like Junia and Prisca, Clare of Assisi, Argula von Grumbach, Mary Bonsanquet Fletcher, and Agnes Ozman. For every Billy Graham there has been an Aimee Semple McPherson. For every Oral Roberts, a Kathryn Kuhlman.

To tell you of all the renewal movements throughout history that centered women would require an entirely different book. One that told the story of the Waldensians who sent female preachers throughout twelfth century Italy, preaching a gospel of repentance. It would be one that spoke of the deep and rich traditions of prominent female leaders in African Christianity—women such as the Kongolese Dona Beatriz Kimpa Vita, who prophesied to her people of the dignity of blackness in an era of colonialism. It would speak of the great church mothers of African American and Latino Christianity who have taught and led and prophesied for centuries, to the glory of God. It would speak of the third century's Perpetua, who disobeyed her father's desire for her to recant her faith, and was consequently martyred for the sake of the gospel.

Today's renewal movements are no different. The church in America is at a crossroads, deciding whether it will follow the ways of power or the way of the Spirit, whether it will be refined as gold in the refiner's fire, or be consumed because of unrepentant sin and corruption. To empower women is to align with the prophetic undercurrent that flourished in the early days of Christianity and has been an ever-present undercurrent in the centuries since. Far from a slip toward cultural capitulation, amplifying the voice and place of women calls us back to something very fundamental about who we are: a peculiar people, called out to model a new way forward of being human. A kingdom way of being human.

At present, allow me to offer several takeaway truth claims followed by concluding thoughts.

A WOMAN'S PLACE IS WHEREVER GOD PLACES HER

The place of women is much debated in churches and, especially, social media. A woman's place is in the home. A woman's place is volunteering in the nursery at church. A woman's place is to submit quietly and listen. A woman's place is to cook, to clean, to bear Christian sons and raise them into Christian men (without, of course, exercising any sort of spiritual authority over them once they've reached adulthood). A woman's place may be on the mission field but certainly not here at home. A woman's place is to create an environment where her man can rest easy so he can go back out into the church and into the world refreshed, with his belly full, his appetites satisfied, and without having his headship questioned. This is the message we have given women, but this is a message from neither the Holy Spirit nor from Holy Scripture.

In egalitarian spaces, without proper empowerment, the message about a woman's place can actually be more discouraging. In explicitly patriarchal spaces, women are told where their place is at the onset. But in disempowering egalitarian spaces, women are invited as equals but often treated as anything but. Disempowering egalitarian spaces tell women she can sit at the "big boy table" if she wants, but she needs to stay quiet—and take the notes for the meeting while she's at it. Disempowering egalitarian spaces tell women they can be directors and coordinators but never pastors. Disempowering egalitarian spaces remain a man's party with women as wallflowers.

One of my favorite spots on the internet for some great egalitarian merchandise is called "Eclectic Egalitarian," run by two Pentecostal friends, Katja and Phil Zarns. One of their designs is called "A Woman's Place is" and it lists out in a punchy fashion precisely what Paul prescribes as a woman's place, principally in Rom 16:

- Deacon
- Generous giver
- Co-worker
- Pastor
- Wife
- Apostle
- Mentor
- Church planter

- Tentmaker
- Dear friend
- Mom
- Teacher
- Sister
- Saint
- Follower of Jesus
- Wherever God has called her[1]

That is precisely the point at hand. A woman's place is wherever God has called her, wherever he places her, whatever he speaks to her. As equals in the church, Christian women are made in the image of the same God, saved by the same cross, and filled with the same Spirit. They do not exist as second-class members of the Christian family who require their spiritual fathers and brothers to arbitrate their callings for them.

No, indeed. A woman is called by *God*, and for a man, *any man* (yes husbands, too) to malign, alter, discourage, prevent, or mistreat that call is a functional heresy. It speaks with our actions that we believe we know better the voice of God for their lives than our sisters. It is a stain on the doctrine of the priesthood of all believers. Those who would moan and groan at this would suggest that letting women lead however they like will bring about chaos within the church. Indeed, empowering women to lead alongside men is the antidote to much of the chaos of the church in this cultural moment. Empowering Christian woman won't result in chaos, but it will result in revival. Sometimes revival in the church feels like chaos to those who stand to benefit from maintaining the status quo.

But a woman's place is wherever God has placed her. And if God has placed her there, the thought of attempting to move her from that place should strike the rest of us with a bit of a holy fear.

A WOMAN'S AUTHORITY IS EQUAL TO MAN

As I've demonstrated in this book, God's created design for men and women is that they would preside as co-priest and co-priestess, stewarding and expanding sacred space. The introduction of patriarchal hierarchy in Gen 3 is as a result of the curse of humanity's rebellion. Jesus broke the curse of the fall by his death and resurrection, thus breaking the bonds of patriarchy.

1. "A Woman's Place Unisex T-Shirt."

Gen 3:16 was undone by John 3:16. This was modeled in the New Testament church, as almost immediately women were elevated in status, both in the church and in the home, resisting the patriarchy and patronage of Roman social and household codes.

What this means for us is that while Gal 3:28 does not erase the reality of differences, including those between male and female, it does prescribe the dismantling of the social implications of those differences within the community of faith. In other words, Paul is not suggesting that, in Christ, men and women cease to be men and women, but rather that the implications of maleness (power and dominance) and femaleness (submission and ignorance) in Roman society have no place in the church, which marches to the beat of an egalitarian drum.

While egalitarians have long-embraced this view *theologically*, living out this view in *practice* has not always been as consistent. It is often easier to default to hierarchy because egalitarian relationships require mutuality, interdependence, communication, humility, and other virtues with which we all often struggle. It is only those who count the cost that recognize the beautiful mess of interdependent relationships is well-worth it. Those of us who have labored hard, though imperfectly and inadequately at times, to cultivate truly egalitarian ministries and marriages can attest to this.

Egalitarianism is not simply *believing* that women and men are equal. A belief that is divorced from action in response to that belief is at odds with the Jewish bosom from which infant Christianity grew. Biblical belief necessitates action that lives into that belief. Thus, egalitarian thought without egalitarian action is patriarchy with only a thin veneer of equality.

It is equally important to note that the social categories we make today—"this is my private life, and this is my business life, and this is my church life"—are a product not of Scripture but of Enlightenment-era thinkers such as John Locke. Early Christians thought more holistically than we do. Therefore, the notion that many egalitarians hold—namely, that women can be equal in status in the church but must be under the covering and leadership of their husband at home—is also void of any true biblical support. It is an inconsistency in Christian living that has for too long allowed us men to feel good about empowering the ladies outside of our homes while maintaining a sense of dominance and power within our homes.

For many men, myself included, this inequality of "egalitarian at church, complementarian at home" was discipled into us as a foregone conclusion. But it is must be reformed and repented of in favor of a more biblically faithful egalitarian holism.

In almost two decades of ministry, I have counseled numerous married or soon-to-be-married couples. Over and over again, the inconsistent application of biblical egalitarianism has been at the root of many (not all, but *many*) of the problems faced by couples. Patriarchy is said to breed order in relationships, but it actually breeds dysfunction. This dysfunction is not because the woman won't "submit" but because, in Christ, the submission is supposed to be mutual. Truth be told, I have observed that couples—egalitarian and complementarian alike—who have the healthiest marriages are ones who are functionally egalitarian. By this, I mean that health and flourishing in interpersonal relationships are encouraged by mutuality, interdependence, sacrifice and compromise, and humility. These qualities make notions like men having the final say or the tie-breaker rule unnecessary, because the couple is in one accord.

THE BRETHREN MUST PASSIONATELY ADVOCATE FOR WOMEN

For the next two subsections, I've chosen the terms "brethren" and "sistren" as a nod to honor two dear friends of Tara and mine, Pastor Ed and Pastor L'Tonia Anderson. They have modeled mutuality in marriage as long as we have known them. They also refer to their three sons, collectively, as "the brethren," which has inspired me to refer our three daughters as "the sistren." They are exceptional role models in both ministry and marriage.

The third truth claim I wish to assert as we part ways at the conclusion of this book is that the brethren—the fathers, sons, uncles, nephews, and male cousins that make up our local churches—must move beyond a passive support of the women in our lives in favor of a passionate advocacy for them. The women in our lives will not often speak up when they feel they are being boxed out or put in a corner. To speak up for oneself when being unjustly treated feels self-aggrandizing and Christian women, especially evangelicals, have often been raised to be deferential—to a man's eyes and thought life, to a man's needs, etc. Thus, simply because the women around you are not saying they need your support, it does not mean that they don't.

We must view our advocacy for women as a virtue and as a calling. It is a virtue because it is something we must cultivate. We cultivate the virtue of advocacy by listening to women, believing women, proactively seeking out feedback, and receiving correction with humility. During my time writing this book on advocating for women, I have made unintentional mistakes in supporting Tara's calling. You can bet you will make mistakes in supporting your loved ones, too. But virtuous advocacy for women is not a matter of how perfectly you do it. As a matter of fact, we need to make mistakes occasionally to remind ourselves that we still have a lot to learn and to avoid developing a savior complex. Instead, virtuous advocacy is the delicate balance between firm support and humble openness. It is the tension of speaking truth to power on behalf of women and also learning how our desire to help sometimes actually disempowers women. It is, to borrow the phrase of Eugene Peterson's so-named book, a "long obedience in the same direction."

Brethren, as you begin to advocate for women you will find yourself facing internal struggles. Your ego will most likely get in the way. Sometimes it will be bruised, sometimes crushed. You will be faced with dilemmas in your workplace of laying aside opportunities that disproportionately default to you so that the women in your organization can have a swing at the bat. You will be forced to wrestle with the ambiguity of how much of the success you enjoy in your career is as a result of your own hard work and merit and how much of it is predisposed toward you because of your gender.

When given the opportunity to give away some of the power you possess to women in your life, it *feels like a loss* at first. It feels like you are giving up a scarce resource. It feels counterintuitive. But Passover power is a part of the upside-down way of the kingdom. The same Jesus who promised that the last shall be first (Matt 20:16) and that loving one's life will result in losing it (John 12:25) is the same Jesus who modeled Passover power (cf. John 13; Phil. 2). It is a power that, when given, returns in dividends. Giving away power to women may feel like a short-term loss, but the return on investment is well worth it. You will undoubtedly find that the benefits of giving away power and opportunity far outweigh any loss, especially as it pertains to the overall health, productivity, and morale of the church or organization of which you're a part.

THE SISTREN MUST SELFLESSLY CHAMPION EACH OTHER

Originally, I had men in mind as the target audience of this book when I set out to write it. But as I spoke with women and heard their stories, and as Tara and others have provided feedback along the way, I have realized that the aims of this book are a significant challenge to the sistren as well.

Sistren, I certainly do not have to tell you how fiercely critical women can be toward one another. A mother need only remember her first pregnancy as a young, expectant mother, who likely received an incessant volley of unsolicited advice with a tone of condescension: "breastfeed or you'll be a bad mom," "bottle feed or you'll forfeit your independence," "you look too matronly in this outfit, but you look too skanky in that one," "oh, you're using an epidural? I could never do that to my baby." And on and on it goes.

This, as you well know, plays itself out in other areas beyond pregnancy. Career choices, ministry choices, clothing choices, hair and makeup choices, parenting choices, etc., are all under near-constant scrutiny—a scrutiny, if I may be so bold to say, you most often inflict upon one another.

What if, dear sistren, you moved from fierce critic to selfless champion? I've watched what a group of determined, equally supportive women can accomplish when they are banded together and disregard the knucklehead stuff about whose jeans are too tight and whose kids are too poorly disciplined. It's a sight to behold. What if elder women in the faith chose to lovingly care for, provide opportunity for, encourage, and practically help their spiritual daughters? What if, rather than criticize a young mother whose child is on a tablet, you offered to watch the child? What if, rather than tearing colleagues down, you advocated for their elevation? What if the sistren recognized that when one of you win, all of you win—and that when one of you win, it is your responsibility to help others win as well?

What could the daughters of the church accomplish if they prophesied arm-in-arm with one another, modeling the selfless way of the kingdom? I believe that while many women do exactly that, we have only just begun to tap into the potential of what Christian women can do when they work together.

WOMEN AND THE FUTURE OF CHRISTIANITY

The future of the church is female.

By this I don't intend to imply that the future of the church isn't male, too, only that it will not be characteristically male. Gina Zurlo, with the Center for the Study of Global Christianity at Gordon-Conwell Theological Seminary did a "World as 100 Christians" study in 2020. The study showed that today the "typical Christian" worldwide is not an American or European middle-class male. Instead, the typical Christian today "is a non-white woman living in the global South, with lower-than-average levels of societal safety and proper health care."[2] This phenomenon will undoubtedly continue to increase as the center of global Christianity continues to grow more into the global South and East.

Within the southern and eastern spaces of global Christianity are movements increasingly led and dependent upon passionate Christian women, who are engaging in God's redemptive mission in the world. We in the West could stand to learn from their example, to let some of that gospel zeal rub off on us and embrace the call that both our sons and our daughters

2. Zurlo, "The World as 100 Christians."

have been called to prophesy as the Spirit impresses upon them. I believe there are at least three ways in which the female shape of the future church stands to benefit its long-term flourishing.

Strengthening Our Unity

When the voice and place of women is elevated within the church, the unity of the church is strengthened. As women are empowered within local churches, as well as Christian businesses and non-profits, they are able to speak for the often-voiceless majority of women in a way that they simply cannot do on the margins. This dismantles the illusion of unity created from the bonds of patriarchy—an illusion maintained only by way of top-down conformity.

True unity flows from the bottom upward and from the margins inward. True unity is when power and privilege seek to safeguard the well-being of and to learn from those who have historically been without power and privilege, be they women, people of color, immigrant groups, the disabled, or the poor. Unity is not when the church puts on a united front to the outside, but when everyone, as the book of Acts reminds us, is of one heart and mind, the meaning of being "in one accord." This is a unity not won easily but rather worked out through the lives of women and men, each devoted to the flourishing of the other.

Cultivating Our Witness

The patriarchal establishment of Rome undoubtedly saw the deconstruction of hierarchies happening within the Christian community as a threat to the Roman way of life.[3] Part of the good news of the gospel for women in the ancient church was that within its community they enjoyed a level of status, authority, and autonomy they did not possess outside of the Christian fellowship. The equality found within the New Testament church was a form of witness—both as a threat to those who benefitted from existing power structures and as a liberation to those who lived as subjects to those power structures. It was a testament to the coming of a kingdom in which all would be liberated from the bonds of sin, both individual and corporate.

Today, the equality that could be afforded to women within local churches could stand as a powerful witness to the liberating truth of the

---

3. See, as another example, Peter Leithart's history of the NT church's undermining of the Roman social order of patron-client reciprocity in Leithart, *Gratitude*.

gospel of Jesus Christ—that, because of the kingship of Jesus, we are invited into a new way of living together. Can you imagine what a witness to the revolutionary claims of the gospel it would be if local churches, who are called to live as outposts of the kingdom, were known as places where women could not simply feel welcomed but could flourish? What would it mean for our witness for the church to be *the* place where women thrive? Where women are cherished? Where women are believed? What if, as it was in Paul's day, the church was where women could go in order to be free?

What would it mean for our witness for our churches to no longer to be places to excuse or conceal the abuse of women but rather fiercely guard them, champion them, value them, and act swiftly and decisively when someone violates them?

The mistreatment of women is a stain on our witness in the eyes of an onlooking culture. One need only peruse the latest news of abuse within churches in America to see how it tarnishes the beauty and purity of the gospel we seek to proclaim and embody. Recovering a gospel faithfulness does not mean pretending like these abuses don't exist in order to "just preach the gospel." Instead, it means dealing seriously with wrongdoing with integrity and righteousness *as well as* addressing the underlying systemic issues that permitted that wrongdoing to happen in the first place. Some have argued that the further empowerment of women should be seen as a capitulation to shifts in culture—in essence, *losing* our distinct gospel witness. And while that sort of fundamentalist fear-mongering may make for a pithy soundbite in a sermon or garner support from the masses on the blogosphere, it simply does not hold water as historical fact.

After all, Jesus believed women. Jesus empowered women. Jesus taught women. Jesus was a safe person for women. Jesus entrusted the news of his resurrection first to women. If being more like Jesus means losing the distinction of our gospel witness, it may be that we are preaching the wrong gospel. The right treatment of, elevation of, and empowerment of women will always serve as a testimony of the liberation, freedom, and beauty we enjoy as citizens of the kingdom of God.

Furthering God's Mission

Finally, as a missiologist, I tend to filter most everything through the *missio Dei* (Latin for "the mission of God"). I'm not simply referring to "mission" in the sense of the unique calling of a missionary who moves to another land and ministering in a culture that is not his or her own. I'm referring to the responsibility we *all* share in God's mission to reconcile humanity to himself through his son Jesus the Christ.

God's mission is the principal and foundational calling of the church. It has been often quoted (and diversely attributed) that "the church does not have a mission; the mission has a church." That means, the mission of God is not simply something the church does as an extension of its broader ministry. It is the entire reason for the church's existence. We are God's missionary people and we partner with God in his mission to reconcile all of humankind unto himself through the lordship of Jesus the Christ.

Why, then, is that a necessary point to make in a book about empowering Christian women? Simply put, if the church is missionary by design, and women comprise more than half of the church, then more than half of the church's missionary force is female. Therefore, how we treat, train, empower, and advocate for the largest missionary segment of the body of Christ matters immensely.

When we place barriers in front of women walking out their calling, when we discourage them, when we put them in a corner, we inhibit their participation in the *missio Dei*. We become stumbling blocks instead of steppingstones. When we discourage women from seeking theological education, when we limit the places and times and audiences in which they can speak, when we limit their opportunities to preach and teach to Mother's Day or to children's churches, we pump the brakes on the steady advancement of the gospel message. It is not enough for men to be proclaimers of the gospel because the truth of the gospel is not male by design. It is, for all who call upon the name of the Lord (Joel 2:32), male and female alike. If its truth be for both male and female, so must its proclamation be. Both our sons and our daughters shall prophesy.

Having grown up a fourth-generation Pentecostal, I heard old, old stories about great women of faith. Many of the best preachers of my youth were old ladies who only needed a microphone and five minutes to bring revival to the land. What I also heard growing up Pentecostal was the immediate need for the whole world to know the gospel. One of the reasons Pentecostalism is one of the fastest growing segments of the Christian population is because it is undergirded by a foundational missional assumption: that the gospel *must* be preached to the ends of the earth. It is not a "when we get around to it" sort of Great Commission. It is a here and now, let's get moving and carry the gospel forward under the direction of the Spirit sort of Great Commission.

Two such examples were two elderly women I knew growing up, who I will call Carol and Louise. Carol and Louise were two women who, if they were married, it was before my acquaintanceship with them began when

I was around five or six years old. Some of my earliest memories in children's church were of Carol and Louise telling stories about their adventures smuggling Bibles into China. They would take little commercial breaks from their stories to do songs with a ventriloquist dummy and other things that Christian kids in the early 90s loved. I remember on more than one occasion they talked about how their age, gender, and rather unassuming nature (they both looked like they would be bringing freshly baked cookies with them, not illegal religious contraband) gave them an edge up when getting through security check points at the Chinese border.

Carol and Louise were always heroes of the faith to me. Though sort of local celebrities within our church for a season, I doubt few will remember them a generation from now. After all, much of the work these women did was intentionally covert. But to think of the lives that were changed because of two women, women who defied the cultural expectations for two single elderly ladies and lived the lives of Bible smugglers in a communist country. If anything, I know they impacted my life for the better. Carol and Louise eventually retired to the Flint area and, though I would see them on occasion while on breaks from college, I eventually lost track of them. But they embodied the feminine mantle of mission better perhaps than any two women I have ever known.

The mission of God is too significant a calling for the church to pigeonhole women like Carol and Louise. It is too great a call to place limits on the callings of half the missionary population that comprises the Christian church. The witness of the church is too precious to squander it on patriarchy. The unity of the church is too important to not amplify the voice and place of women so that they may be rightly represented and empowered within the body of Christ.

Too much is at stake. The mission is too important. The women of the church must be permitted to rise up and prophesy as the Scriptures command. Let us then take up the holy mantle to come alongside them—to advocate for them, to lift up their voice, and to see that they have every opportunity to walk out the calling laid upon their lives.

Let's do it for my three daughters.

For your daughters.

For all the daughters of the church.

Bibliography

Barr, Beth Allison. *The Making of Biblical Womanhood: How the Subjugation of Women Became Gospel Truth.* Grand Rapids: Brazos Press, 2021.

Barrett, C. K. *A Commentary on the First Epistle to the Corinthians.* New York: Harper & Row, 1968.

Baxter, Judith. *The Language of Female Leadership.* London: Palgrave Macmillan, 2010.

Bond, Sarah E. and Shaily Patel. "Recovering the Female Clerics of the Early Church." Jan 17, 2022. https://bit.ly/3GowZK1.

Burge, Ryan (@ryanburge). "Here's membership statistics from 1987–2020." Twitter, Jun 30, 2022, 10:56 a.m. https://bit.ly/3YLA65z.

Carter, Joe. "3 Steps Christian Institutions Take from Orthodoxy to Sexual Immorality." The Gospel Coalition. https://bit.ly/3YJKn2g.

Church of God (@COGHQ). "Bylaws Amendment III." Twitter, Jul 22, 2022, 5:36 p.m. https://bit.ly/3FQyDCD.

Crouch, Andy. *Playing God: Redeeming the Gift of Power.* Downers Grove: IVP, 2013).

"Defining DEI." University of Michigan. https://bit.ly/3HX3HD8.

Etsy.com "A Woman's Place Unisex T-Shirt." https://etsy.me/3PRGXqo.

Foster, Richard J. *Money, Sex & Power: The Challenge of the Disciplined Life.* 1st ed. San Francisco: Harper & Row, 1985.

Du Bois, W. E. B. *The Souls of Black Folk* in *Three Negro Classics.* New York: Avon, 1965.

Georges, Jayson. *Ministering in Patronage Cultures: Biblical Models and Missional Implications.* Downers Grove: InterVarsity, 2019.

———. *The 3D Gospel: Ministry in Guilt, Shame, and Fear Cultures.* N.p.: Timē, 2014.

———. "Back To God's Village." Jan 23, 2014. YouTube Video, 4:40. https://bit.ly/3H4nhdS.

Gregoire, Sheila Wray. "15 Things That Kill a Woman's Libido." Bare Marriage. June 6, 2022. https://bit.ly/3PQfqoV.

———., and Keith Gregoire. *The Good Guy's Guide to Great Sex: Because Good Guys Make the Best Lovers.* Grand Rapids: Zondervan, 2022.

Heiser, Michael S. *The Unseen Realm: Recovering the Supernatural Worldview of the Bible.* Bellingham, WA: Lexham, 2015.

Hiebert, Paul. *Transforming Worldviews: An Anthropological Understanding of How People Change.* Grand Rapids: Baker Academic, 2008.

Hoekendijk, J. C. *The Church Inside Out.* Philadelphia: Westminster, 1966.

Imes, Carmen Joy. "Helper: You Keep Using That Word for Women." *Christianity Today*, Aug 30, 2022. https://bit.ly/3FQdDM7.

Keener, Craig. "Women in Ministry." Sep 25, 2019. YouTube Video, 46:16. https://bit.ly/3WiYl9V.

———. *The IVP Bible Background Commentary: New Testament.* Downers Grove: InterVarsity, 1993.

Korpi, Todd. *The Life-Giving Spirit: The Victory of Christ in Missional Perspective.* Skyforest, CA: Urban Loft, 2017.

Lamm, Ari (@AriLamm). "Why Read The Bible In Hebrew?" Twitter, Aug 19, 2022, 8:56 a.m. https://bit.ly/3YLNyq3.

Leithart, Peter J. *Gratitude: An Intellectual History.* Waco, TX: Baylor University Press, 2014.

Low, Robin. *Good Intentions Are Not Enough: Why We Fail at Helping Others.* New Jersey: World Scientific, 2016.

Madigan, Kevin, and Carolyn Osiek. "Ordained Women in the Early Church: A Documentary History." *New Blackfriars* 90.1025 (2009) 131–35. https://onlinelibrary.wiley.com/doi/epdf/10.1111/j.1741-2005.2008.01258_2.x.

Manetsch, Scott M., ed. *1 Corinthians.* Reformation Commentary on Scripture: New Testament IXa. Downers Grove: IVP Academic, 2017.

McKnight, Scot, and Laura Barringer. *A Church Called Tov: Forming a Goodness Culture That Resists Abuses of Power and Promotes Healing.* Carol Stream, IL: Tyndale House, 2020.

Mowcko, Marg. "Tertullian on Equality and Mutuality in Marriage." Marg Mowczko, Sep 4, 2016. https://bit.ly/3BWJIRg.

Morgan, Anna. "Best Practices For Developing Female Leaders in Egalitarian Churches." Literature Review, Fuller Theological Seminary. Unpublished, 2019.

Mullen, Wade. *Something's Not Right: Decoding the Hidden Tactics of Abuse and Freeing Yourself from Its Power.* Carol Stream, IL: Tyndale Momentum, 2020.

Myers, Bryant L. *Engaging Globalization: The Poor, Christian Mission, and Our Hyperconnected World.* Mission in Global Community. Grand Rapids: Baker Academic, 2017.

Nouwen, Henri J. M. *Reaching Out: The Three Movements of the Spiritual Life.* 1st Ed. Garden City, NY: Doubleday, 1975.

"Obituaries: Berniece Matejcek." MLive. May 20, 2017. https://bit.ly/3ORf28T.

The Office. Season 3, Espiode 15, "Phyllis' Wedding." Directed by Greg Daniels, written by Caroline Williams. Aired Feb 8, 2007 on NBC.

Peppiatt, Lucy. *Rediscovering Scripture's Vision for Women: Fresh Perspectives on Disputed Texts.* Downers Grove: InterVarsity, 2019.

Qualls, Joy (@madamspeaker). "COG—Cleveland Sisters." Twitter, Jul 27, 2022, 7:48 p.m. https://bit.ly/3YLoqjl.

"Queen Bees: Do Women Hinder the Progress of Other Women?" BBC News. Jan 4, 2018. https://bbc.in/3jendAL.

Rah, Soong-Chan. *The Next Evangelicalism: Releasing the Church from Western Cultural Captivity.* Downers Grove: IVP, 2009.

Reese, Randy D., and Robert Loane. *Deep Mentoring: Guiding Others on Their Leadership Journey.* Downers Grove: IVP, 2012.

Richards, E. Randolph, and Richard James. *Misreading Scripture with Individualist Eyes: Patronage, Honor, and Shame in the Biblical World.* Downers Grove: IVP Academic, 2020.

———., and Brandon J O'Brien. *Misreading Scripture with Western Eyes: Removing Cultural Blinders to Better Understand the Bible*. Westmont: InterVarsity, 2012.

Rohr, Richard. *Eager to Love: The Alternative Way of Francis of Assisi*. Cincinnati: Franciscan Media, 2014.

"The Role of Women in Ministry." Assemblies of God. https://bit.ly/314haR2.

Salvatierra, Alexia. *Faith-Rooted Organizing: Mobilizing the Church in Service to the World*. Downers Grove: InterVarsity, 2014.

Smietana, Bob. "Saddleback Church Ordains Three Women, Defying Southern Baptist Convention." *Washington Post*. May 5, 2021. https://wapo.st/3VlobZv.

Sunquist, Scott. *Understanding Christian Mission: Participation in Suffering and Glory*. Grand Rapids: Baker, 2013.

Villacorta, Wilmer. *Tug of War: The Downward Ascent of Power*. Eugene, OR: Cascade, 2017.

Villodas, Rich. *The Deeply Formed Life: Five Transformative Values to Root Us in the Way of Jesus*. First edition. Colorado Springs, CO: WaterBrook, 2020.

Walton, John H. *The Lost World of Adam and Eve: Genesis 2–3 and the Human Origins Debate*. Downers Grove: IVP Academic, 2015.

———. *The Lost World of Genesis One: Ancient Cosmology and the Origins Debate*. Downers Grove: IVP Academic, 2009.

———., et al. *The IVP Bible Background Commentary: Old Testament*. Downers Grove: InterVarsity, 2000.

Welcher, Rachel Joy. *Talking Back to Purity Culture: Rediscovering Faithful Christian Sexuality*. Downers Grove: IVP, 2020.

The West Wing. Season 1, Espiode 12, "He Shall, From Time to Time." Directed by Arlene Sanford, written by Aaron Sorkin. Aired Jan 12, 2000 on NBC.

Wright, Christopher J. H. *Truth with a Mission: Reading Scripture Missiologically*. Grove Biblical Series 38. Cambridge, UK: Grove, 2005.

Wright, N. T. "Biblical Basis for Women's Service in the Church by N. T. Wright." Mar 29, 2017. YouTube Video, 58:27. https://bit.ly/2G23vDd.

Yeh, Allen. "'Give Us Friends!': V. S. Azariah and the Call for the Four-Self Church." *Evangelical Missiological Society Journal* 26 (2018): 3–23.

Zurlo, Gina A. "The World as 100 Christians." Gordon-Conwell Theological Seminary. Jan 29, 2020. https://bit.ly/3HSKmTM.